MW01703096

Kinesthetic Voice Pedagogy

Motivating Acoustic Efficiency

by

Kenneth W. Bozeman

Inside View Press

Kinesthetic Voice Pedagogy

Motivating Acoustic Efficiency

By Kenneth W. Bozeman

ISBN: 978-0-9905073-6-9

www.voxped.com

Inside View Press
676 Founders Ridge Drive
Gahanna OH 43230

Contents

Foreword

Anyone who has had the good fortune of attending one of Ken Bozeman's workshops, or of speaking with him about his work, knows what kind of infectious passion he has for acoustic pedagogy. Between breaks at conferences, over a meal, or in the throes of workshops, he is always happy to share his understanding, and truly wants us to understand the topic—to take what is good about our work and have it become even better. Following the success of his first book, this latest study not only gives us more depth of information, but also outlines ways to apply the work directly in the studio. He took *Practical Vocal Acoustics* and made it…well, more practical.

Whether new to teaching or already well established in your work, we all have much to learn from Ken and from his example. He continues to learn and explore voice pedagogy with a sense of wonder, humility, and excitement—open to every possibility, and as much a student as a master. That may be exactly what makes him such a compelling role model, and why we would do well to follow his example. I have sat attentively in the front row of his presentations, taking copious notes, shared his writings with my students, reworked certain studio practices as a result of the information, and just tried to keep up. Ken's writing and research shows the caring and experience of a career in the voice studio. His ability to relate theoretical information to pedagogical application is a particularly winning combination, and helps us with the primary focus of our work—the practical, hands-on, day-to-day work we do with students.

This beautifully crafted, well-written book is part of a storied pedagogical tradition, and carries the torch in the truest spirit. Ken is mindful to honor and build solidly on the writings and best traditions of the past to help facilitate a pedagogy that points the way forward. He finds a way to bring together the traditional tried-and-true with a contemporary empathy and understanding.

The text is bookended with a focus on the importance of expression, and the sincere impulse of communication is a running theme. It becomes unmistakable that he is interested in the whole singer—the kinesthetic, hearing, thinking, feeling, and fully expressive artist. From the focus on expressiveness, to Western classical singing, to speech, to strategies more appropriate for other styles of singing, his work is straightforward and clear. When he reminds us about the central importance of emotion, he is supporting us in our work to facilitate artistry. As he writes about remapping the open throat, he is also inviting us to have an open mind. Indeed, the mapping both of the body and of how we might use the strategies in the studio becomes a treasure map of the very best kind—one that might just lead to buried vocal treasure.

Ken, thank you for teaching us, and for furthering the cause by helping us to teach others. We are the richer for it. Your work not only adds to our understanding, but is also an important stepping-stone in continuing to move the profession forward. Like the sage advice offered in the conclusion, this current work partners with historic *bel canto* ideals to allow the voice to be as vibrant and as fully expressive as our imaginations will allow…

Norman Spivey
Professor of Voice and Voice Pedagogy, Penn State
Immediate Past President, National Association of Teachers of Singing
Member, American Academy of Teachers of Singing
January 2017

Preface

Since the publication in 2013 of *Practical Vocal Acoustics: Pedagogic Applications for Teachers and Singers*, interest has continued to grow in acoustic pedagogy and its application. This has been manifest in a steady stream of requests to explain and demonstrate its principles at various universities and for events sponsored by the National Association of Teachers of Singing. In the summer of 2015 twenty-five singers and teachers assembled for a weeklong seminar on acoustic pedagogy at Lawrence University's Bjorklunden Lodge in Door County, Wisconsin with the author and voice scientist Christian Herbst. This seminar will be periodically repeated as long as interest persists.

Subsequent to the publication of PVA I have continued to realize further implications and applications of acoustic pedagogy, about which I have been encouraged to write as a followup to the first book. In particular, teachers want to know how to translate refined acoustic understanding into the more subjective, kinesthetic, and preferably simpler guidance needed in the studio. This present account is in response to that interest. It draws (with permission) on two articles that were published in the interim, one in the *Journal of Singing* and the second in the NYSTA e-publication *VOICEPrints.*

Many earlier writers in voice pedagogy based their vocal advice on traditions handed down filtered through their personal "clinical" experience in the studio. In a field dependent upon creative motivation of physical response—which also must contend with the unpredictability of human response to stimuli—identifying reliable, repeatable strategies across singer populations is challenging, even if what constitutes good singing were clearly agreed upon. The more recent reliance of writers on the scientific method to sort fact from fiction has seemed, to some, to neglect the art and psychology of the motor learning training task. Some earlier, descriptively framed strategies (e.g., inhaling through a smile; the *coup de glotte* onset; etc.) were neglected or even rejected, perhaps prematurely, in favor of implications from emerging science or of changing pedagogic views. Very recently renewed attention has been given to earlier pedagogy, such as is found in James Stark's *Bel Canto: A History of Vocal Pedagogy,* Michael Trimble's *Fundamentals of Great Technique,* and Daniela Bloem-Hubatka's *The Old Italian School of Singing,* and championed in the *Journal of Singing* articles of Stephen Austin, and the blogs of David Jones, to name but a few. The necessity of kinesthetic terminology for studio application has been emphasized by authors such as Karen Bauer, emerita professor at North Park University. Bauer's book, *The Essentials of Beautiful Singing: A Three-Step Kinesthetic Approach,* highlights this need and then offers well-conceived, fact-based kinesthetic instruction.

This text focuses on kinesthetic strategies for realizing acoustic efficiency. It should be reiterated that acoustic pedagogy is but one piece of the overall pedagogic puzzle. There are clearly other crucial fronts that must be addressed in the training of singers. Nonetheless, in my experience, improved understanding of vocal acoustics and especially of acoustic registration can transform one's problem-solving effectiveness in the studio as much or more than any other single area. To be sure, it must be coordinated with, and in most cases preceded by, effective instruction about breath management and laryngeal registration, and it is best motivated by means of genuine expressive, affective stimuli.

I must acknowledge a significant further refinement in our understanding of vowel perception and vowel modification—with valuable insight into application—that has been contributed by Ian Howell, head of vocal pedagogy at the New England Conservatory of Music. My own understanding, adaptation, and incorporation of Ian's work is summarized in chapter four, Vowel Perception, Modification, and Motivation, and referenced throughout much of this text. This refinement, while compatible with my prior understanding, supplies valuable new specificity and has led to very practical perceptual advances in studio application. For a more precise understanding of the implications of Howell's work, see his dissertation document, the link to which is listed in Selected References, p. 84.

My pedagogic journey and current working conclusions are based on and indebted to at least three sources:

1. Respect for and interest in the best of historic pedagogy, especially the Italian *bel canto* traditions as reported by a number of recent authors (James Stark, Stephen Austin, Michael Trimble, Daniela Bloem-Hubatka, David Jones, to name a few) and also as summarized by the late Richard Miller as the international Italian school. This respect extends as well to historic descriptive terminology (terms such as head voice, chest voice, *voce chiusa, voce aperta,* closing, cover, *chiaroscuro,* etc.). As new terminology is added, most historic terminology needn't be discarded, only appropriately qualified and understood.
2. Ongoing, emerging information from voice science, especially work in voice acoustics (drawing from the work of Johan Sundberg, Ingo Titze, Donald Miller, and others). Though I did not personally drink from his stream, Berton Coffin must be acknowledged as a pioneer among voice teachers in applying voice acoustics to pedagogy. Others have also contributed to this body of knowledge (Vennard, Appleman, etc.).
3. Awareness and use of innate and/or evolved responses of the human body and psyche: yell; whoop; yawn; the biomechanics of regurgitation; the Valsalva maneuver; response of the respiratory system and vocal tract to the impulse to communicate; the effect of emotion or expression on vocal tract poise and voicing; to name a few. These strong, preprogrammed responses should either be recruited or, when necessary, effectively countered in the training of singing.

Readers who have previously digested the information presented in *Practical Vocal Acoustics: Pedagogic Applications for Teachers and Singers* will be in the best position to understand the recommendations made in this short volume. This text assumes that exposure and refers to principles previously explained there. *Kinesthetic Voice Pedagogy: Motivating Acoustic Efficiency* is therefore considered a sequel and companion piece to the former. While the applications and recommendations of this text venture beyond what is scientifically established, they are intended to be grounded in a fact-based pedagogy, whose objectives have been established and affirmed by convergences of the three foundations cited above.

I direct the reader to several online resources for future reference:

1st: the Facebook page for Practical Vocal Acoustics (occasional announcements are made there concerning presentations and resources):

https://www.facebook.com/acousticvocalpedagogy

2nd: the resource website for *Practical Vocal Acoustics* (this site has multiple resources for teaching voice pedagogy and will be periodically augmented as appropriate over time):

http://www.kenbozeman.com

3rd: the author's personal website (information about the author and his schedule of presentations, residencies, and workshops will be kept up to date there):

http://faculty.lawrence.edu/bozemank/

Finally, a personal thanks to the following: Ian Howell, Carol Mastrodomenico, Matthew Edwards, Martha Randall, and Joanne Hayes Bozeman for valuable feedback on drafts and chapters; artist Christopher Bozeman, for help with graphic illustrations and the cover adaptation; Norman Spivey both for feedback and for his gracious foreword, and Scott McCoy for his encouragement and assistance in publishing this book.

Sincerely,

Kenneth W. Bozeman
Frank C. Shattuck Professor of Music
Lawrence University Conservatory of Music
Appleton, Wisconsin
December, 2016

About the Author

Kenneth Bozeman, tenor, Frank C. Shattuck Professor of Music at Lawrence University Conservatory of Music in Appleton, Wisconsin, (1977-present) holds performance degrees from Baylor University and the University of Arizona. He subsequently studied at the State Conservatory of Music in Munich, Germany on a fellowship from Rotary International. He is chair of the voice department at Lawrence, where he teaches voice and voice science and pedagogy.

Mr. Bozeman has received both of Lawrence University's Teaching Awards and was awarded the *Van Lawrence Fellowship* by the Voice Foundation and NATS in 1994 for his interest in voice science and pedagogy. He is currently the chair of the editorial board of the NATS *Journal of Singing*. He is a frequent presenter on voice acoustics—especially as applied to male *passaggio* training—for venues including the Voice Foundation, the Physiology and Acoustics of Singing Conference, the Pan European Voice Conference, and the European Voice Teachers Association, and various NATS venues: the 2012 and 2014 conventions, the 2015 Winter Workshop, and an online chat in January 2016, and as a master teacher for the 2013 and 2017 Intern Programs. His book, *Practical Vocal Acoustics: Pedagogic Applications for Teachers and Singers,* is used in many voice pedagogy courses. Mr. Bozeman was an active recitalist and performer of oratorio, having performed with the Milwaukee Symphony, the Wisconsin Chamber Orchestra, the Green Lake Music Festival, the Louisville Bach Society, and on Wisconsin Public Radio. His students have sung at major opera houses, including Deutsche Oper Berlin, New York City Opera, Santa Fe, Houston Grand, San Francisco Opera, Chicago Lyric, and the Metropolitan Opera.

Chapter 1

Introduction

Overview of the Task

The publication of *Practical Vocal Acoustics: Pedagogic Applications for Teachers and Singers* represented an attempt to explain in accessible terms the vocal acoustic landscape that singers inhabit, its tendencies, challenges and inherent pedagogic implications. Though several chapters enumerated various implications, recommended strategies, and offered exercises, subsequent reader response has requested more elaboration and examples of practical application. Legitimate questions came, such as, "How does one translate acoustic background information into studio directives?" Or, "How soon do you present challenging acoustic concepts to your young singers?" The latter question invites the tease, "Well, that depends on how soon you want your young males to stop yelling their top notes?" Of course, the background information a teacher needs to know, and what that teacher says to the student are rarely the same thing. Furthermore, detailed work on vocal acoustics is best attempted only after a healthy breath to voice connection is begun and basic flow phonation is established in at least the lower middle voice.

A more serious response to both questions acknowledges that knowing the vocal acoustic landscape and even understanding its pedagogic implications does not automatically reveal the more subjective, kinesthetic directives one needs in the studio. Teachers need to know how to stimulate vocal tract behaviors and tunings now known to be favorable. This requires that one translate objective acoustic goals and causes into the subjective, kinesthetic, operational motivations and perceptions of the singer. This text demonstrates effective kinesthetic strategies for realizing clear physiologic and acoustic objectives.

Vocal Motivation

Studio pedagogy requires that we understand what motivates phonation in the first place. What follows is less a review of scientific investigations of that question than a collection of informal observations and working conclusions of the author. A foundational assumption is that voice—from its inception—has been motivated by emotive expression and the impulse to communicate, eventually realized through evolved language patterns.

Expressional Motivation

Voice is motivated almost exclusively by the impulse to communicate, usually including expressive, emotional elements. Very few voiced sounds are not expressively motivated (exceptions include reflexive coughing, sneezing, hiccups, and throat clearing). The pitch contours of inflected speech are spontaneously generated by communicative expression. Singing is generally thought to be a response to an even more intense, heightened communicative impulse. Sung sounds are therefore most successful when expressively motivated. Pitch, intensity, duration, and inflection are all the result and realization of an expressive trajectory and journey. One could say that melodic notation is really a kind of symbolic choreography of specific expressions. The task of the singer then involves a kind of reverse engineering, in which she intuits and executes the sequence and progression of expressions that will result in the pitch contours, dynamics, and durations given by the composer.

Linguistic Patterns

The sounds of language have been learned with their meanings, inflective patterns, and inherent expressive qualities, through imitation of one's caregiver models. The child then wills and pre-hears a meaningful sequence of language sounds in order to guide the subsequent vocalization. Idiomatic linguistic groupings and word stress guide the contours of the resultant inflection. Vowel quality becomes more challenging when voicing at pitches beyond typical speech range, where normal speech shapes yield vowels that no longer exactly match the expected speech level sounds. Singing routinely calls for vowels outside of—usually above—typical speech level frequencies. Yet in Western classical singing there is a general aesthetic expectation of intelligibility as well as of beauty and projection. The Italian counsel of "*si canta come si parla*" ("one sings as one speaks"), while generally applicable, does require qualification. This is especially true at higher frequencies, for the simple reason that one does not speak at the high frequencies routinely called for in singing.

Organizing Principle

Considering the variations across range brought about by the changing acoustic interactions of pitch (and resultant harmonic sets) with vocal tract resonances (formants), and the complexity of the things that must be coordinated, the student will need some unifying, organizing principle to simplify her motivation and integrate the various necessary factors. Singers cannot and should not try to micro-manage the many tasks simultaneously at play in skillful, artistic singing. Once basic mechanics have been rehearsed, affective expression can be just such an organizing, integrating motive. In this manner, the impulse to communicate with its particular emotive quality stimulates the pre-phonatory set up of the vocal tract and folds, the manner of inhalation, the onset of sound, and its continuation in an inflected, expressive phrase shape. Though thoroughly rehearsed in prior practice, such motivation can achieve an innate, genuine spontaneity.

General Orientation: Inhalation & Pre-Phonatory Tuning

Much good can be done before a sound is made. Indeed, much good *must* be done before voicing starts, that is, both before and during inhalation. General structural support *before,* and pre-phonatory tuning *during* inhalation set the body and voice up for best function and resonance. These factors, which are simultaneous with inhalation, ideally should be in response to the impulse to communicate. Balance and alignment of the body, and especially of the torso, free the respiratory system for efficient reaction to the needs of the voice.

Pre-phonatory tuning of the torso and vocal tract can be built on hard-wired, innate responses of the body to the impulse to express. These involve both preparatory patterns of inhalation in the torso, as well as the muscle tone and poise of the vocal tract in response to feelings. It has recently been reported by Michael Trimble (*Fundamentals of Great Vocal Technique,* Insideview Press, 2013) that earlier *bel canto* pedagogies were built on the inhalatory pattern of a baby preparing to laugh or cry (i.e., to express itself) rather than on the relaxed respiration of a baby resting or sleeping. In this expressively activated mode, the lower abdominal musculature is already engaged, providing some resistance to the visceral pressure of a descending diaphragm, and thereby directing more of the expansion toward the lower back, in contrast to the relaxed frontal expansion of the lower abdomen used in resting inhalation. In this manner both the torso and the pharynx are motivated by expressive impulse and are immediately poised for phonation, eliminating the need to reset a lax abdomen in order to phonate. As long as the singer is not hyperfunctional in torso or pharynx by nature or habit, has not habituated an upwardly heaved chest, and can therefore allow a sufficiently full, downward inhalation, this enlivened, innate response is very effective. Inhalatory expansion into the lower back also activates sufficient tracheal pull to settle the larynx for best function. Though abdominal resistance during inhalation is contrary to much breathing pedagogy of the last half century, it has these advantages:

- It is consistent with the idea of phonation (and its preparatory inhalation) being motivated by the innate response of the body to the impulse to communicate.
- It eliminates the extra step of breathing in a non-communicative, at rest mode, before subsequently activating abdominal muscles for singing.
- It correlates and coordinates simultaneously and more instinctively with an expressive pre-phonatory poise of the pharynx, in contrast to complete abdominal release and bulging, which tends instead to trigger laxity and drooping in the pharynx and palate.
- For all of the above reasons, it integrates the torso and entire vocal apparatus in an instantaneous readiness for expressive voicing.

Convergent *Chiaroscuro* Setup

The acoustic goals of Western classical singing are best achieved with a resonator/filter that is generally convergent in shape, that is, one that is relatively open in the laryngopharyngeal area, and narrower somewhere further downstream, in the oral cavity or closer to the lips. Such a strategy provides the necessary context for achieving the singer's formant cluster, and therefore assists in creating the *chiaroscuro* timbre (balance of ring and depth) considered ideal to Western classical singing. It also increases beneficial interactivity or non-linearity, in which resonance feeds back helpfully on the vocal folds, assisting their efficiency. This is accomplished via the time honored "open throat" being properly executed, plus sufficient closeness of vowel articulation. The following chapter offers reliable, effective strategies for achieving such a shaping.

Sensation Sorting

Singers sing largely via sensory perception and recall. In selecting kinesthetic directives to achieve better function, specifically better shaping of the vocal tract for acoustic efficiency, the teacher and singer must take into account and differentiate among several overlapping sources of sensation. There is a kinesthetic awareness of where things are in the vocal tract in the first place. Then there are the sensations of shaping for singing—how the singer perceives the shaping of the vocal tract, specifically the lips, tongue, degree of jaw opening, soft palate position, and laryngopharyngeal openness. There are sensations of acoustic vibration that change from vowel to vowel and across range as harmonics move through formants or formants through harmonics. There are the sensations of muscular action and the degree or absence of muscular effort. If hearing is considered as a sensation, there are the changing sensations and perceptions of tone and vowel color across range. And finally, there may also be changes in the physical feel of expression stimulating the pitch change, since inflection is motivated by the communicative progression of expression across an utterance or phrase. These various sensations complicate the singer's perception of what he or she is doing or not doing, requiring some sorting. For example, when a singer is attempting to maintain vocal tract shape and level of effort to facilitate passive vowel modification across range, as the pitch is raised, both the vowel quality and the resultant acoustic feedback sensations will migrate, so much so that it may feel like the shape itself is being changed. Awareness and anticipation of the migratory paths of both vowel color and of the changing vibratory feedback can assist in maintaining appropriate vocal tract stability. Sensations of expression, shape, and acoustic vibration are welcome and can be useful. Sensations of laryngeal effort and subglottal pressure should be minimal to non-existant. The singer will need to discover kinesthetic motivations that can provide appropriate stability, yet allow appropriate mobility, in other words, that maintain those things that should stay the same while allowing those things that must change or migrate the freedom and flexibility to do so.

Studio Technology

Given the increasing use of studio technology that can display realtime acoustic feedback and analysis, a statement about its value and limitations seems in order here. This author first experienced realtime spectrography in the late 1980s and has used it continuously in his studio since the early 1990s. It is as ever present as the mirror on the wall over the piano. Like the mirror, it is utilized only when needed to supplement explanations and to point out clearly observable phenomena, such as continuousness of line, vibrancy and overall general resonance. In many lessons it has been ignored altogether, and it has never been allowed to dominate the lesson atmosphere. However, it can provide valuable additional feedback as an audio playback device with a fairly intuitive visual representation of the sung sound.

Teachers who truly understand acoustic pedagogy and are able to accurately identify its timbral causes and effects can effectively apply its principles in lessons *without* such technology. Indeed, if they cannot apply acoustic pedagogy without technology, they probably cannot do so with it. Good teachers can also teach effectively without the use of a mirror or sound playback devices. However, most would not choose to deprive themselves of such useful feedback devices for those times when their use improves studio efficiency. Realtime spectrography—in the hands of someone who understands its uses and limitations—can be a valuable additional feedback device.

Chapter 2

Remapping the Open Throat *(Gola Aperta)*

(Adapted and reprinted with permission from the *Journal of Singing*)

Richard Miller began a section in *The Structure of Singing* entitled *The Open Throat (Gola Aperta)* with the following statement: "It would be hard to find a teacher who recommended singing with a closed throat."[i] While some voice teachers avoid addressing the issue directly, experience and reason suggest that most teachers advocate the proverbial "open throat." At least two excellent articles addressing this topic have previously appeared in the *Journal of Singing* (Miller and Kenny[ii], Austin[iii]). The directive to have an open throat goes back at least to the writings of the early Italian pedagogues, all of whom recommended singing with *una gola aperta.* Specifically, the Italian school pedagogic literature maintained that "inhaling through a smile" or as if "inhaling the fragrance of a rose" opens the throat.

Concerns with Open Throat Directives

In contrast to the general agreement about the value of having an open throat, concerns about directives and/or conscious attempts to open the throat also exist. The smile directive recommended above is thought by many teachers to be excessively lateral and to cause a "spread tone" and therefore, if used at all, has been supplanted by "inner smile" imagery. Richard Miller, an advocate of the international Italian school of singing, raised concern in the chapter cited above about the use of yawn imagery by some to open the throat:

> In the literature of vocal pedagogy can be found sources that advocate as the ideal position for singing exactly the fully distended pharyngeal and buccal posture found in the yawn.[iv]

Then later:

> To breathe as though inhaling deeply the fragrance of a rose is to accomplish the buccopharyngeal position of *gola aperta,*

> in direct contrast to techniques of the open throat achieved through the yawn.[v]

Others echo the concern that a throaty, swallowed tone can result from attempts to open the throat. Some speech language pathologists are leery of open throat directives as being contrary to the frontal vibratory feedback typically sought in resonant voice therapy.

Anatomic Realities

In pursuit of fact-based pedagogy, let's examine what the situation really is. First it must be noted that the muscles that open the throat are not in the throat. Indeed, there are no muscles that can directly expand the pharynx.[vi] All pharyngeal muscles are termed constrictors for a reason: when activated, they narrow or constrict the pharynx. Since the spinal column is directly behind the back throat wall, unless the spine itself is contorted it is not possible to distend the pharynx posteriorly, perception to the contrary notwithstanding. The only muscle actions that in some sense actually open the throat are:

- relaxing the pharyngeal muscles
- elevating the soft palate from above
- lowering or settling the larynx from below
- fronting the tongue
- decompressing the thyrohyoid space
- retracting or deconstricting the false vocal folds

The Challenge: False Kinesthesia

The principle challenge to effective throat opening is this: our kinesthesia (sensory awareness) of throat space is misleading—in fact, it is exactly backward. If you ask a group of people which vowel *feels* the most open-throated, most will cite /ɑ/, or which vowel the most closed-throated, most cite /i/. This is indeed the way it feels. If asked to inhale through their most exaggeratedly open-throated sensation, most people will make a yawny /ɑ/, which upon inhalation will be accompanied by a moderately loud turbulent noise and cooling in the laryngopharynx (perceptual throat). Paradoxically the throat is rather narrow in the /ɑ/ and at its most open posture with the vowel /i/, primarily due to the difference in tongue shape and tongue fronting of those vowels.

Noiseless Inhalation

When the throat is in the instinctive but false open-throated feeling upon inhaling, the inhalation is noisy and there is a cooling sensation in the throat behind the tongue, precisely where the narrowing occurs. This results from the necessary increase in air speed at the narrowing and the resultant turbulence and cooling from both windchill effect and evaporation at that location. If the student reshapes the vocal tract to move the cooling to the front of the mouth, the tongue will have been fronted and the throat will be more open.

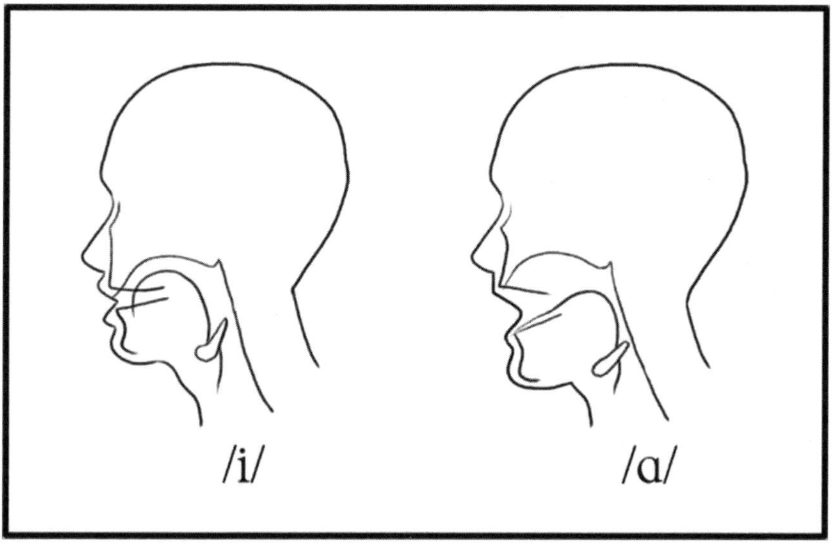

Figure 1: Saggital View of the Vocal Tract in the Vowels /i/ and /ɑ/.

Resonator Convergence

Recent observation and hypothesis in vocal acoustic science suggest that classical singers prefer a resonator shaping that is as convergent as the vowel and pitch being sung will allow (Titze[vii]). This hypothesis proposes that resonator convergence assists in establishing the desired classical *chiaroscuro* timbre, which manifests in a depth-dependent singer's formant cluster.[viii] Singer's formant cluster—as modeled by Sundberg[ix], Titze, and Story[x]—requires a low larynx and a laryngopharynx that is six times larger than the opening of the epilaryngeal exit. This causes formants three through five to draw together, mutually boosting each other. Convergent shaping also contributes to vocal tract inertance, which can interactively assist the vibrator, all of which can boost the power of the entire signal (ring *and* depth) for less breath pressure. Resonator convergence is therefore dependent upon some openness of the laryngopharynx.

First Formant Location

Acoustically, an open throat has a lower first formant. The lower the first formant frequency is for any given vowel (within acceptable diction and comfort), the more open the throat, the deeper the timbre, and the more convergent the resonator shape. Therefore if the "pitch" of any perceived noise is lowered, throat space will have been increased. The approximate pitch and timbre of the first formant can be heard by means of the noise created by inhaling or exhaling with the vocal folds in near adduction as in an /h/, as long as the larynx has not been raised, that is, in a modified whisper. Both formants one and two may be heard in a whisper—the more open the throat, the more the first formant will dominate the noise, the narrower and shallower the throat, the more the second formant will dominate the noise.

[Caution: whispering is typically done with a raised larynx and narrowed laryngopharynx in order to increase and highlight the noise of the second formant, which is perceptually associated with vowel clarity.]

Body Mapping

Accurate body mapping also can help. By way of review, body mapping—an offshoot of Alexander Technique—is the observation that we each have an internalized conceptual "map" of how the body is put together: where things are, where joints are, how they articulate—in other words, of how the body works. Body mapping theory suggests that inaccurate mapping leads to awkward use, while accurate mapping facilitates better coordination. Because our kinesthesia is backwards for throat space, it seems plausible that most people have inaccurately mapped the location of the back of the throat and the insertion and function of the tongue.

The Back Throat Wall

When experiencing the false open-throated sensation described above, the back wall of the throat seems to be located further back than it actually is—as if it is behind the ears. In fact, the back throat wall is in front of the ears. (I suspect that what we are perceiving in this maneuver as the back of the throat is in fact activation of that lateral part of the tongue muscle group, the styloglossus, that retracts the back of the tongue.) If while inhaling we remap our concept of the back throat wall to its actual location in front of the ears, we will have fronted the tongue and opened the throat.

Mapping the Tongue

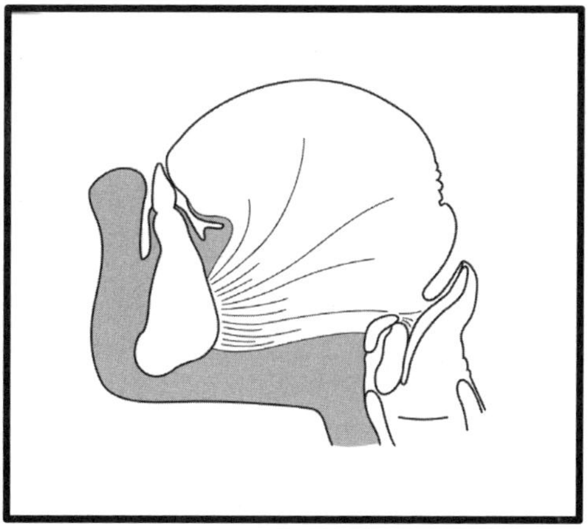

Figure 2: Accurately Mapping the Genioglossus (the largest part of the tongue muscle)

Furthermore, we also tend to incorrectly map the tongue as forming a somewhat rounded 90° angle that lies flat in the mouth and then courses down the throat vertically to attach to the larynx. While there are some lateral (hyoglossus) attachments to the hyoid bone below, the largest portion of the tongue muscle (the genioglossus) loops back to the front under the tongue blade where it originates on the inside back of the chin. When relaxed, the tongue is fronted, somewhat rounded, and usually in contact with the roof of the mouth rather than lowered and flattened. Remapping the tongue from running down the throat to folding back under itself to the chin will allow the tongue to be fronted and relaxed and the larynx to be more independent from the tongue. The sensation of pushing the larynx down from above is also false. Muscles cannot push. They can only pull their ends toward the center or pull toward the end of their more stable attachment (their origin). Activating the lateral hyoglossus muscles lowers the back of the tongue and pulls up on the hyoid bone, compressing the tongue into the hyoid bone, possibly even raising the larynx. This helps neither voice acoustics nor laryngeal independence and freedom of function. Try correctly remapping the back throat wall and the tongue shape as described earlier and inhale through this new mapping. The jaw need only release and drop as far as temporomandibular joint (TMJ) rotation alone allows (i.e., without jaw translation)—about a finger width. You should experience cooling in the front of the mouth rather than behind the tongue, and a noiseless inhalation, both of which indicate an actually opened throat.

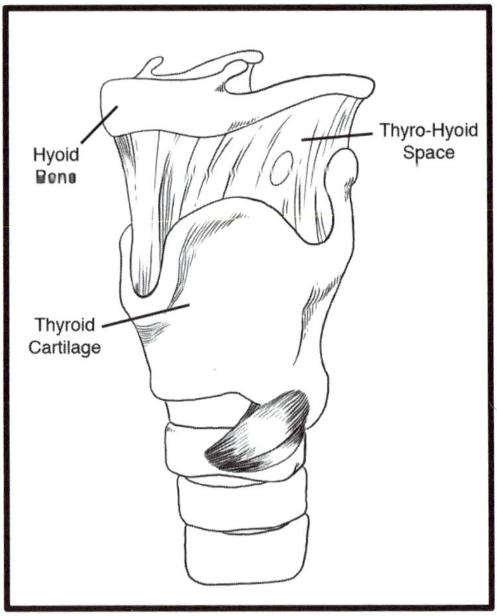

Figure 3: The Thyrohoid Space

The Thyrohyoid Space

The swallowing muscles that raise the larynx compress the throhyoid space. Maintaining a stable laryngeal position on the other hand leaves the thyrohyoid space loose and open. This can be monitored—in students whose anatomy lends itself to easy identification of laryngeal structure—by gently palpating the thyrohyoid space toward the back of the larynx on either side. It should remain open and not rise or become smaller with pitch ascent. Though this space varies in size among individuals, it may also have been reduced in size by residual tension from unnecessary, habitual activation of swallowing muscles during speech production. If such behavior is entrenched, it should be patiently countered and broken, preferably through speech therapy with a licensed speech pathologist familiar with appropriate therapies. Effective strategies include massage and stretching of the thyrohyoid space, and monitoring the looseness and openness of the thyrohyoid space during speech production, inflective sirens or loops, and sung glissandi.

Glottal Suction Therapy

A compressed thyrohyoid space can be safely stretched by a glottal suction therapy as follows: with the glottis firmly but comfortably closed, the student should activate inhalatory effort in the torso, creating a subglottal suction that pulls the closed glottis downward from below. This can be assisted by exhaling below the resting level of lung volume before closing the glottis, generating passive inhalatory recoil—the lower the lung volume, the stronger the passive inhalatory recoil. Take care to keep the glottis closed, not allowing any air through. Since—with the exception of the glottal closure—this is an inhalatory gesture, the structures surrounding the area (false vocal folds, pharynx) will be disinclined to contract or compress the throat; rather there is a general opening and stretching around and within the larynx. Several benefits ensue: the thyrohoid space is stretched, the false vocal folds are retracted, the larynx is lowered with no activation or depression of the tongue, complete glottic closure and competence are safely strengthened, and inhalatory muscles are exercised against resistance, an important aspect of breath management for pressure reduction. This maneuver is most effective if balanced from above by a "pharyngeal grin" or smile, which prevents its composite action and sensation from being exclusively in a downward direction. (See Use of Affect immediately below) Furthermore, glottal suction tends to simultaneously stimulate palatal height. This may be related to regurgitation programming: in regurgitation, abdominal pressure is increased by simultaneous contraction of abdominal muscles and the diaphragm, pressure is reduced in the chest around the esophagus, and the glottis is closed and palate raised to direct the flow out the mouth. Therefore, starting a phonation with a gentle glottal onset immediately after a glottal suction stretch maximizes glottis to palate vertical height.

The Use of Affect to Open the Throat

Voice is almost exclusively played by expression. This is hard-wired from birth. The first thing a baby does is to take a breath. The next thing most babies do is to apply that breath to their vocal folds and let you know how they feel about what just happened. This communicative connection to vocal coordination seems to apply to the entire system, including the poise and posture of the vocal tract. We can use this. Furthermore, an inhalation should simultaneously be an inspiration of the feeling one is about to express. If upon inhalation the student uses appropriate affects to stimulate a better pharyngeal posture, the throat can be opened in a more spontaneous manner. Affects that have proven effective in the studio for opening the throat include: suppressed laugh[xi]; mischief; being pleased with oneself; empathy; and sympathy (many more are possible). Combining the accurate remapping mentioned above with an inhalation inspired by an appropriate motivational affect should result in a noiseless inhalation, and an open throat poised for best resonance. In this regard, this author suspects that the early Italian teachers' directive to "inhale through a smile" has been misunderstood. A deep, genuine smile is perhaps more about its inner pharyngeal effect than its outer facial or lip effects. A "pharyngeal grin" felt in the nas- and laryngo-pharnx rather than the oropharynx, can both open and stabilize the throat in a favorable poise. Maintaining the sensation of a strong pharyngeal smile is a safer, innate way to avoid throat closure across changes of laryngeal registration and to facilitate appropriate vowel migration across range.

Articulation and "Placement" Sensations

For the lower and middle voice ranges at least, having a fairly close articulation from vowel to vowel assists in keeping the throat open, the first formant lower, the resonator convergent, and the timbre *chiaroscuro.* Though sound cannot actually be placed, there is a possible basis for variation in sensation of vibration along the vocal tract, due to the pressure nodes of the resonated sound waves. Awareness of a vibrational locus in the mouth, usually along the hard palate and above, according to the image in Figure 4 can assist with maintaining an open-throated, *chiaroscuro* timbre.

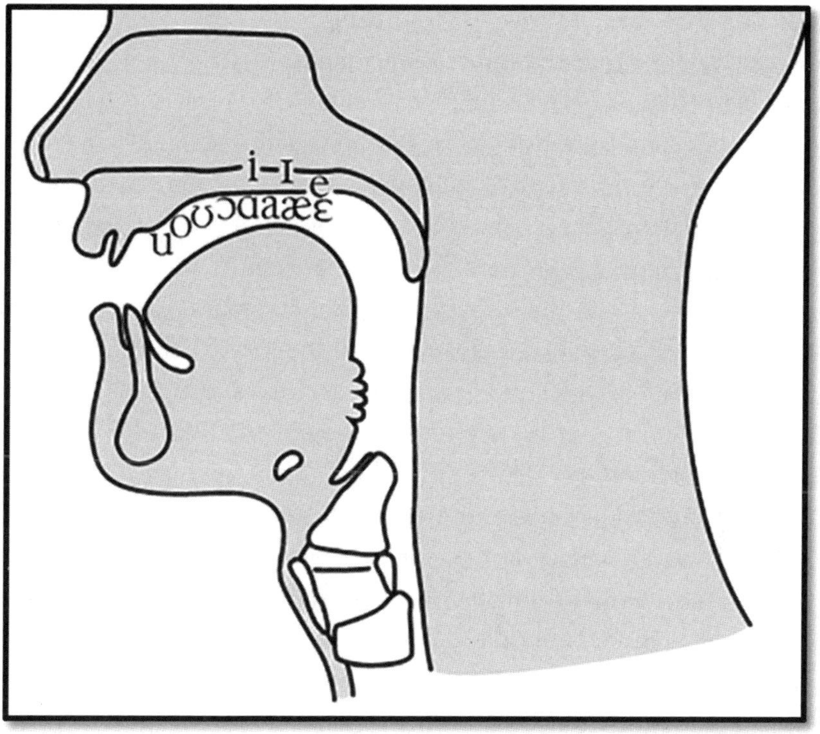

Figure 4: Second Formant "Placement" Sensations

These vibrational sensations are associated with the changing frequencies of the second formant. Paradoxically, the front vowels are felt further back and the back vowels further forward. There is also some sense of "placement" location relative to the vocal tract dividing tongue hump: front vowels, involving a fronted tongue hump, have a vibrational locus slightly behind the tongue bulge, while back vowels, with a bulge more to the rear, are perceived more in front of the tongue hump on the hard palate. (See Figure 4).

[*Nota bene:* all of these sensations are along and above the hard palate, and therefore relatively frontal. Furthermore, tonal acoustic sensations are comprised of various components given the multiple vocal tract resonances and harmonics at play. Second formant sensations along the hard palate are but one of these perceptual facets.]

Maintaining an Open Throat Across Range

The instinct to approach the upper range as in a "yell" is universal and strong. This behavior is an instinctive tracking of the second harmonic by the first formant by means of a shorter and increasingly divergent resonator. It is accomplished by activating swallowing muscles to raise the larynx and narrow the pharynx, and by frontal opening of the vowel. Overcoming this innate response is a major concern of Western classical vocal training. To avoid this behavior upon ascending the range, males should stay in fairly close vowel posture until the vowel being sung turns over—that is, until the second harmonic surpasses the first formant, achieving close timbre—and a bit beyond. Thereafter, in order to maintain robust timbre and avoid whoop timbre, vowel opening *within* close timbre can commence. (Whoop timbre occurs when singing the pitch of the first formant, or when the first formant is tracking the pitch one is singing.) If care is taken to stay in close timbre (to keep the first formant [F_1] below the second harmonic [$2f_0$]) and to avoid raising the larynx, some opening of the vowel shape at this point does not compromise an open throat.[xii] Treble voices desiring a headier quality (women and countertenors) should stay in close timbre until the pitch of the first formant (and "whoop" timbre) is attained. Above that pitch, vowel opening to track the fundamental frequency with the first formant (to maintain whoop timbre) is necessary for full classical head voice timbre, but care should still be taken not to raise the larynx except for extreme high range, at ca. B5 and above.[xiii]

Conclusion

An open throat is a desirable pedagogic goal for free, resonant singing in Western classical timbre. However, since kinesthesia for throat space is typically misleading, care must be taken in choosing the directives given to accomplish an actually opened throat. The use of noiseless inhalation which cools the front of the mouth, accurate mapping of the location of the back wall of the throat and of tongue insertion and function, appropriate inspirational affects, relatively close vowel articulations for resonator convergence, and awareness of second formant "placement" sensations can be effective strategies to accomplish and maintain an actually opened throat and *chiaroscuro* classical timbre.

Chapter 3
Studio Metaphors for Acoustic Pedagogy

(Adapted and reprinted with permission from the
NYSTA ejournal, *VOICEPrints*)

Vocal Tract Acoustics

The vocal tract is a quarter wave resonator with multiple natural resonances—that is, frequency peaks at which it is more responsive to input from voice source harmonics. Any harmonics introduced by the vocal folds into the vocal tract that are near those frequency peaks will excite more sympathetic vibration from the air contained in the vocal tract. In other words, source harmonics near vocal tract resonances will be significantly amplified or boosted (resonated) and radiated to the outside world, while harmonics farther away from resonance peaks (in the valleys between peaks) will be suppressed. Effective vocal resonance is about maintaining some of these resonances (the overall location of the entire formant set and of the singer's formant cluster) for timbral consistency by stabilizing the vocal tract length, while tuning the first two resonances—also called the vowel formants—for maximum output. The first (or lower) formant is perceived to be associated more with the vertical pharyngeal column and timbral depth, and the second with the oral cavity and vowel definition and clarity. In Western classical technique having some degree of convergence of resonator shape—limited by the vowel and pitch being attempted—improves resonance balance between the high and low frequencies within the timbre and increases beneficial acoustic feedback on the vibrator (vocal folds), improving glottal efficiency.

The Need for Kinesthetic Terminology

Though accurate as an explanatory, general framework of what needs to happen, the description just given does not help the student know specifically what to do or how to do it. In seeking idealized resonator shapes, the student faces the challenge of adjusting one part of the vocal tract without inappropriately affecting another part, especially when moving away from habituated speech shapes, as is often necessary in active vowel modification. For example, mouth opening can trigger larynx raising, since both are coupled in the instinctive yell response. Voice teachers must therefore translate their knowledge of effective formant tuning into accurate vocal tract mapping strategies and the most likely subjective kinesthetic perceptions of the singer—in other words, from the spatial arrangements that we know need to happen to what the student needs to think in order to generate those behaviors. A kind of body mapping exercise that has proven helpful in this author's experience follows.

A Two Room Metaphor

The vocal tract is divided into two "rooms" by a tube-narrowing bulge of the tongue dorsum toward a location somewhere along the palate. The "back room" is the vertical pharyngeal column, with the glottis as its floor and the soft palate as its ceiling. A narrowing caused by a tongue bulge toward the hard palate creates a dividing inner threshold into a "front room" formed by the oral space extending from that tongue bulge to the teeth and lips. The teeth and lips then form a "front door" to the outside world. With this vocal tract mapping metaphor in place, various directives have proven useful.

Perception Deception

As mentioned in the previous chapter, perception can be misleading. A clear example of this involves our perception of the tongue, throat space, and the location of the back of the throat. An open throat is universally recommended for classical *chiaroscuro* timbre. However, what is also seemingly universally perceived as an open throat—the "yawny" /ɑ/—is in fact a throat narrowed by a posterior tongue bulge, and what is felt to be a narrowed throat—the /i/ vowel—is in fact the most open throated vowel posture. (See Figure 1, p. 9) The felt location of the back throat wall in a yawny /ɑ/ seems rather far back, somewhere behind the ears, an anatomical impossibility. The actual back throat wall is in front of the ears and cannot be expanded further back (without changing the neck and spinal posture) because the spinal column is there. What we are probably feeling as throat expansion (a false kinesthesia) is the activation of the styloglossus muscles, those lateral tongue muscle strands that course posteriorly to the styloid processes just below and in front of the ear canals and that retract the tongue body into the pharynx. If you attempt a full yawn, you can feel this muscle action toward your ears. Singers should avoid this degree of back sensation in their singing. So, ***the distance from front to back should be perceptually short.*** A sensation of great length from lips to the back wall—like the sensation of space directly in the back of the mouth toward the spine—is false and evidence of a tongue being retracted into the pharyngeal column, narrowing the throat—perception notwithstanding.

Furthermore, as mentioned in the previous chapter, the main tongue body is felt to be shaped like an "L" or an angle iron, that lies flat in the mouth and then makes a rounded 90 degree angle down the throat to the larynx, to which it seems attached. While it is true that some outer, lateral portions (hyoglossus) of the tongue muscle complex descend and attach to the hyoid bone, the largest part of the tongue muscle (the genioglossus) folds back under the tongue blade where it originates from the inside back of the chin. (See Figure 2, p. 11) Remapping the location of the back of the throat to its actual location in front of the ears, and the tongue body as a folded muscle that attaches to the chin releases the styloglossus and fronts the tongue, increasing pharyngeal space, or opening the throat.

Directives for the Two Room Metaphor

For classical timbre ***there should always be two rooms*** in the singer's perception, even on the least convergent (i.e., most divergent) vowels. This is accomplished by always having some sense of narrowing between the rooms, that is, of keeping the tongue bulge relatively close to the hard palate. ***Keep the threshold between the two rooms as close and high as the vowel and pitch will allow.*** This accomplishes enough internal convergence of resonator shape to assist *chiaroscuro* timbre, even when the front room is divergently shaped for the particular vowel. The jaw and tongue should be free, but minimally lowered for open or back vowels. For close vowels, the jaw will need to open sooner with ascending pitch, but the tongue height should remain relatively high. For men this opening of the closest vowels commences well before reaching the pitch of the first formant in order to *avoid* whoop timbre. Open vowels can stay in close position rather high. While there should be no sensation of holding or inhibiting the jaw, greater openness is only needed higher in the range for the open vowels. For treble voices, in order to maintain and track whoop timbre, opening commences from the pitch of the first formant of each vowel.

Conversely, if the tongue is lowered too far, especially in the middle voice, the perception will change from two rooms to that of one room, extending from the back wall to the opened mouth. This may be an appropriate strategy for belt timbre, but is not as helpful for classical timbre. The acoustic consequence of a "one room" sensation will tend to be a less gathered, collected and a more "spread" timbral sensation.

Directives for the "Back Room"

The back room should always be tall, with the floor (the larynx) comfortably low and the ceiling (the soft palate) high, both with some sense of lateral width. The front wall of the back room (actually the back of the tongue) should also be felt to be as tall as the vowel allows, eliminating depression of the back of the tongue. This arrangement is best accomplished via the use of appropriate affects. A strongly activated affect—such as a smile, mischief, pleasure with oneself, suppressed laugh, or strong empathy/pathos—stabilizes the overall vocal tract length and actually opens the throat by fronting the tongue. While the back room contributes to both ring and depth, it is especially responsible for depth of timbre. An appropriately low laryngeal position facilitates ease and efficiency of laryngeal registration across range. In keeping the inner threshold narrow, take care that the back room is not collapsed; rather, it should be stretched taller. An alternative image is the inverted megaphone, with the small end at the narrowed threshold (the tongue bulge toward the palate) and the large open end just in front of the ears.

As explained above, the back room isn't really that far back—it is in front of the ears. When well opened, it feels tall, laterally open, but paradoxically somewhat slender from front to back. Remember that ***the sensation of backspace is notoriously false***, and is most likely the sensation of activating the styloglos- sus—of backing the tongue into the throat. This is easily proven by the noisy inhalation that accompanies that sensation, as well as the cooling wind chill effect precisely where the throat has been narrowed. An open throated inhalation cools the front of the mouth, not the throat.

The Back Room Is Not Back

Since the back throat wall is in front of the ears, the "back" room or pharyngeal column is actually in the front half of the head and in the front third of the neck. Perhaps a more accurate designation for this space would be the "middle" room, but then there is no room behind it. It is therefore helpful to remember that the back room is centrally located rather than in the back of the head. Furthermore, since preoccupation with the back wall directly behind the mouth can stimulate tongue lowering and the false kinesthesia of back space, it is best to remember to keep the perception of the location of the back wall of the back room as forward as is comfortably possible. Plainly stated, the back room is not back, it's in front of the ears.

Perceptual Sense of Self

While a person's emotional center may be seem to be in the chest (near the heart), one's sense of personal agency is typically located in the center of the head behind the eyes, more or less in the vicinity of the ears—in other words, near the top of the back room. This is perhaps due to the location of the centers of hearing, sight, and balance. Once the singer is aware of this "place from which" they perceive and interact with the world, they should determine to ***"stay in the back room"*** just inside the inner threshold (tongue bulge), and not to travel out into or center themselves in the front room perceptually. This can be very effective in re-enforcing good structural alignment and in avoiding a reaching forward of the face or jaw either for expression, ascending pitch, or changing vowel.

Directives for the "Front Room"

Do not darken or color the front room. The front room is all about vowel clarity and ring. It should be perceived to be in front of the singer's sense of self. The front room is like a sunroom—light, clear, and ringing—and should not be used to color, darken, or deepen the tone. As the primary factor tuning the second formant, it is responsible for the clarity of all vowels and the defining quality of vowels other than /u/ and /o/.

Front Vowels: If the vowel is a tongue-fronted vowel (the so-called front vowels: /i ɪ e ɛ/), the front room can feel rather exposed and be as divergently shaped from the tongue hump forward as the vowel will allow. The perceived vibrational locus of the front vowels is paradoxically at or just behind the threshold between the rooms—in other words just above and/or behind the tongue hump. (See Figure 4, p. 15.) Since front vowels are situated just inside the vertical back room, and the threshold between the rooms is kept relatively high and close, the back room will supply sufficient depth of timbre. Therefore the front room should be divergent enough to supply a complementary clarity, with no lip rounding over the teeth to warm or darken the timbre.

Back Vowels: When singing a lip rounded back vowel /u o ʊ ɔ/, the mouth should be kept in as close a posture as is comfortable, with the jaw minimally dropped, until the singer has reached the pitch of the first formant (treble voices) or well above the pitch of turning (non-treble voices). These back vowels are perceived to vibrate more in the front room on and above the hard palate. It is as if there is a short, small tube in the front room through which the vowel rings. If the oral cavity is sufficiently small, the lips merely form a continuation of the tube's roundness, and needn't round further nor pull down to cover the front teeth. The closeness or convergence of vowel shape is maintained in large part via the strength of the affective[1] posture (pharyngeal grin) that is stabilizing the palatal height and pharyngeal length. In keeping the front room small, take care not to collapse the ceiling height of the back room (the soft palate). Keep a strong inverted megaphone sensation or inner pharyngeal grin affect. Back vowels therefore triangulate somewhat, with a low floor (glottis) and high ceiling (soft palate) in the back

[1] Please refer to *Definitions*, page 76, for a discussion of the use of affect

room, plus some forward vibratory sensation on the hard palate in the front room.

No vowel should seem to be directed toward the back wall. Even the front vowels, which vibrate near the top of the back room just inside the tongue hump, should stay close to that threshold. And back vowels, though also needing a tall back room, should have a primary vibrational locus on the hard palate of the front room.

Open & Central Vowels: The vowel /ɑ/, with its inherent divergence, challenges the two room perception. The tongue bulge should be kept (by means of affect) as close to /i/ as is feasible, with back and front rooms as open as that narrowing will allow. A resonant /ɑ/ will seem to vibrate in the threshold, between the tongue hump and the palate, and may sound modified toward a ringing /ʌ/, especially to the singer. With open and central vowels /æ a ɑ ʌ/, given their more divergent tendencies, it is helpful to center them just inside the tongue bulge, maintain the vertical height of the back room, and sense acoustic feedback both above the mouth and below the tongue in order to avoid a "mouthy," one-room orientation. Finally, with ascending pitch all vowels will seem to include in the singer's perception a greater degree of the timbral quality of the first formant. With these adjustments, ***all vowels can seem fairly close together,*** especially in the lower and middle voice.

Strength of the Pharyngeal/Laryngeal Affect

Keep the pharyngeal affect strong. The degree of the affective muscle action that stabilizes the pharynx and larynx can be rather strong. Like yawning, it can do no physical harm, no matter how strongly activated, since it is self-limiting, but it is preferable to the yawn for resonator tuning, since yawning distorts the timbre by backing the tongue into the pharynx. The pharyngeal affect should not be relaxed for softer or higher sounds, rather should be stronger. Affective poise of the vocal tract is typical and instinctive in strong spontaneous expressions. This stabilizing use of affect helps to keep the throat open and the resonator convergent, and to gather or collect the sound sensation, creating the perception of acoustic narrowing or "closing" through the *zona di passaggio*. It does not result in a tight or constricted sensation—rather a strongly expressive, possibly even firm poise. It is a satisfying, communicative sensation, not a laborious, unpleasant one.

Vowel Modification

As harmonics approach and cross the first formant, there is inevitable *passive* vowel modification or migration. This occurs with *no shape change*. When it becomes necessary to open the mouth or jaw farther (either to avoid whoop timbre in men, or to track whoop timbre in treble voices), the vowel is then being *actively* modified. Men need active modification primarily for the close vowels /i y u/, and occasionally mid-close vowels such as /ɪ e ʊ o/, since they do not sing pitches as high as the first formants of open vowels. More often, however, males need to allow the passive vowel migrations that occur with pitch ascent while maintaining *stable* vocal tract shapes, especially at the change from open to close timbre, where the second harmonic rises through the first formant.

Keeping the vocal tract shape the same is more easily said than done, since its shape is normally guided by our concept of the target vowel sound. As we hear the vowel passively migrating, we instinctively want to counteract and "fix" it by opening the vowel, which can trigger laryngeal elevation and throat narrowing. It is helpful to be very familiar with the predictable passive vowel migrations that occur with pitch ascent in order to allow them to occur without shape adjustment.

For treble voices (females and countertenors), as the sung pitch approaches the first formant, the vowel will passively achieve maximal migration as it arrives in whoop timbre. This migration is often inappropriately avoided via vowel opening and throat narrowing. However, for example, if a soprano keeps the vowel shape sufficiently close, an /o/ will gradually migrate toward an /u/ starting at about A4 and arriving at about C5. This should be encouraged in order to maintain a truly open throat. Treble singers are usually surprised at how what sounds to them like an /u/ is still a convincing, if close /o/ to the external audience. Most vowel migrations sound more modified to the singer than to an external listener.

Typical Student Errors

Relaxing/Collapsing the Pharyngeal Affect: this typically causes a lowering of the sensation of tonal "placement" from on and above the palate to lower in the mouth. It can also cause the soft palate to droop. This often occurs when attempting quieter dynamics, when moving from a front vowel to a back vowel, and with upward leaps. In the attempt to keep the inner threshold sufficiently close, it can also occur that both pharyngeal affect and tallness, and front room divergence are collapsed. A change in facial expression either toward neutral/deadpan or eyebrow raising introspection often accompanies this collapse of affect and inner laxity, as does a subtle tipping up of the head away from level.

Moving into the Front Room: the perception of personal agency moving forward into the front room typically accompanies a lowering of the tongue hump and some degree of movement of the face up and forward. This error typical of back vowels (whose vibrational locus should be felt on the hard palate in the front room) can create the perception that one is changing places with the vowel; if the singer's personal center of agency moves to the front room, the vowel moves to the back room.

Creating One Perceptual Room: this also occurs by dropping the tongue bulge so much that the vocal tract feels like one divergently shaped room, narrow at the back and open in the mouth (whether or not the lips are rounding). A divergently shaped resonator—depending upon how it is done—is a more appropriate acoustic strategy for styles related to belting. This behavior also can collapse the palate and move the singer's self-perception forward from the back room. With lip-rounded vowels a one-room perception creates a large, hollowed oral sensation, accompanied by excessive lip rounding to cover the upper teeth, which reduces ring.

Under Opening Close Vowels: close vowels need to be opened earlier (lower), before the sung pitch reaches the first formant to avoid whoop timbre and retain virile timbre for men, or from the first formant on up to maintain whoop timbre for treble voices where the first formant tracks the sung pitch. Paradoxically, in order to be resonant, the close tongue vowels—especially /i/—will need to be *more* opened by the jaw than an open vowel such as /ɑ/ in the upper middle and upper voice. However, though the jaw opens farther, the tongue bulge should remain high, the larynx low, and the inner threshold narrow to preserve the vowel identity and timbral depth.

Over Opening Open Vowels: Open vowels can stay in close, speech-like posture until the sung pitch reaches the pitch of the first formant, especially for treble voices. Males (other than countertenors) don't reach the pitch of the first formants of the open vowels, but may open vowels above the turn in order to tune the second formant to a higher harmonic. Treble voices only reach the first formant of open vowels near the top of the treble clef.

Darkening the Front Room: insufficient divergence, by not opening the jaw enough when appropriate, not getting the lips out of the way, covering the teeth with the lips, enlarging and hollowing the mouth/front room, or by retracting the tongue tip reduces the ring of the sound or interferes with better formant tuning, reducing overall resonance. For lip rounded vowels in the lower and middle voice, keep the mouth space small (short, small tube), the acoustic sensation high on the palate, and use minimal lip rounding. The "placement" perception of lip-rounded vowels is kept higher on the palate with sufficient affective motivation, such as mischief, amusement, or being pleased with oneself. For non-lip rounded vowels, don't lip round. For these the lip muscles are passive, and are shaped instead by the expression on the face, which should almost never be a deadpan droop; rather, the facial expression should reflect some sincere, even if light, expressive motivation. We are not programmed to make expressive, resonant sound from lax, deadpan motivation.

Conclusion

Training the tuning of the vocal tract to promote best resonance for each vowel across all pitches of the range poses pedagogic challenges. Not the least of these challenges is how best to motivate vocal tract shapes that yield acoustically necessary, nuanced passive vowel migrations or active modifications not usually experienced in the speaking range. The "two room" metaphor has proven to be a body mapping exercise that effectively helps students sort and shape the various components of the vocal tract for improved resonance.

Chapter 4

Vowel Perception, Modification, and Motivation

Vowel Formation and Definition

It has long been understood that vowels are defined and differentiated primarily by the tuning of the first two formants of the vocal tract. It was therefore assumed that modifications or changes of the vowel required changes in the tuning of those two formants by means of changes in the shape of the vocal tract. What was not understood until more recently is that changes of pitch (and therefore of the entire set of harmonics of a tone) cause changes in vowel perception independently of shape changes of the vocal tract. This is due in part to the changing relationships between moving source harmonics and a stable vocal tract formant structure. As pitch ascends and source harmonics rise in frequency through the first formant, the amplitudes of those source harmonics increase and decrease as they ascend into and then through the formant peak. This causes the timbre of both voice and vowel to become increasingly closer until whoop timbre is reached, where the sung pitch equals the frequency of the first formant. With the pitch's arrival into whoop timbre, the vowel will have maximally migrated. These vowel migrations occur with no change of the vocal tract shape. They are caused by the change of pitch. In *Practical Vocal Acoustics* this was labeled *passive* vowel modification in contrast to the *active* vowel modification that is accomplished by changing the shape and thus the formant tuning of the vocal tract. In short, maintaining the shape of the vocal tract while changing the sung pitch will result in a migration of the vowel quality toward a closer neighbor upon ascent and a more open neighbor upon descent.

Recent Developments in Vowel Perception Theory: Absolute Spectral Tone Color

In *Practical Vocal Acoustics,* the first formant was reported as being responsible for timbral depth and the second formant for vowel clarity. More recent investigations by Ian Howell, head of pedagogy at New England Conservatory, suggest further refinements to vowel perception theory.

This emerging understanding maintains that individual harmonics have **absolute spectral tone colors**—that is, vowel-like qualities—such that lower frequency harmonics have an /u/-like quality, slightly higher harmonics an /o/-like quality, higher yet, an /ɔ/-like quality, continuing through an /ɑ/, /a/, /æ/, /ɛ/, /e/, eventually to an/i/-like quality when near 2000Hz (see Figure 5).

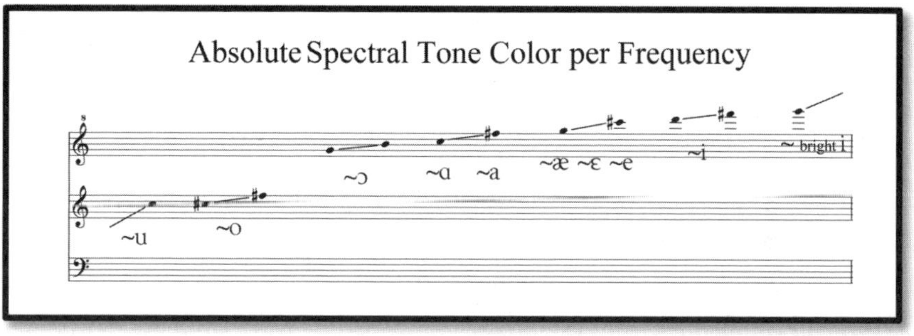

Figure 5: Absolute Spectral Tone Color of Harmonics by Pitch (adapted from Ian Howell, with permission)

Each of the first two formants (the so-called vowel formants) typically reinforce from one to several individual harmonics, each with an inherent absolute spectral tone color. If a formant's bandwidth is reinforcing two or more harmonics, the perceived vowel quality contributed by that formant would be that of an imagined harmonic lying at the **spectral centroid** (an amplitude weighted average of the harmonics) of the amplified harmonic set, closest to the strongest harmonic. In this way, each vowel formant contributes a vowel-like tone color. Our ears then perceive these two vowel quality components as being blended into the composite vowel. This is somewhat analogous to the blending of two primary colors into a new color (blue and yellow into green), to arrive at the composite, externally perceived vowel. Since the first formants of all vowels live primarily within the treble clef, and therefore within some portion of the /u/ (ca. 500 Hz or lower), to /o/ (ca. 500 -700 Hz) absolute spectral tone color frequency range, occasionally venturing into /ɔ/ range, the first formant contributes a warming, rounding, deepening /u/ or /o/-like quality to every vowel. The second formant, being closer in frequency to the absolute tone color of all target vowels other than /u/

or /o/, is more responsible for the clear, differentiating and defining quality of the final vowel complexes of the remaining vowels. The blended result is affected not only by the frequencies of each composite formant contribution, but also by the relative intensities of each formant-enhanced harmonic group. The stronger the first formant contribution, the warmer, deeper, rounder, and more modified the vowel will be. The stronger the second formant contribution, the clearer, brighter, less modified, and if excessive, shallower and more shrill the result.

While the entire vocal tract participates in setting the locations of all of its resonances, the first formant is most influenced by, and perceived to be primarily located in the pharyngeal area, especially the lower pharynx and could be perceived as an "under vowel" component. The second formant is both actually and perceptually associated with the oral cavity and sensations along the hard palate and above, and could be perceived as an "over vowel." A second formant dominant sound therefore can have a "mouthy" orientation and quality; while a first formant dominant sensation has a "back room" (mid-head, in front of the ears) orientation and more vertical perceptual quality. A balance between these two components is desirable.

The Special Case of /u/ and /o/

The vowel defining roles of the first two formants are reversed for /u/ and /o/. Since the second formants of /u/ and /o/ lie in the absolute tone color range of /ʊ/ and /ɔ/ respectively, they cannot account for the defining identity of those vowels. However, the *first* formants of /u/ and /o/ *can* define them, in that the harmonics being featured by their first formants have precisely the absolute tone colors of /u/ and of /o/. In other words, the first formants (under vowels) of /u/ and /o/ play both the expected role of supplying depth (roundness, warmth) *and* the atypical role of defining the vowel identity for those two vowels. The second formants (over vowels) on the other hand, rather than defining /u/ and /o/, contribute clarity and projection, as they also do with all other vowels. (See Figure 5, p. 29.)

The phenomenon of absolute spectral tone color also helps to explain why, of the two closest vowels /u/ and /i/, the /u/ loses identity sooner (lower) with the vowel opening necessary for active modification during pitch ascent. The defining quality (absolute tone color) of an /u/, which is provided by the first formant of the voice, does not exist above C5. The first formant of tones sung above that pitch can only be comprised of harmonics with the tone colors of more open vowels. By contrast, since the defining quality of the vowel /i/ is provided by its *second* formant, which lies well above any pitches one is likely to sing, its identity can be preserved much higher, even with the mouth opening of active modification, as long as the tongue dorsum can remain sufficiently close to the roof of the mouth. Jaw opening does eventually lower the second formant, compromising /i/ identity when in extreme treble range (ca. A5 and above).

Balance of Timbral Elements

Beautiful singing requires an effective balance of these two vowel elements. In general, the higher the sung pitch, the more the singer will need to allow the spectral tone color of the first formant to increase in his/her perception via stable open-throatedness, while at the same time maintaining the oral shape necessary for the clarity and ring of the second formant. The former objective involves maintaining the tall, laterally open, but slender front-to-back pharyngeal sensation that accompanies an open throat. This pharyngeal sensation can be approximated as a sort of vertical rectangular shape whose top "corners" are just inside the temporomandibular joints (soft palate raising area), whose bottom "corners" are to either side of and below the base of the larynx, near the top of the sternum, and whose back wall is in front of the ears. The singer should neither collapse the sense of inner smile, grin, or empathy (the top corners) that accompanies an expressively lifted palate, nor sense the bottom of the throat as narrowing into a point in the larynx, which would be indicative of excess throat closure and squeeze. In the author's experience, this approach is similar to what is intended by the pedagogic advice of the Italian *bel canto* school to open the throat by inhaling through a smile or as if "inhaling the fragrance of a rose." Though the latter (fragrance inhaling) image involves some opening of the nasopharynx by fronting the lifted soft palate a bit, it nonetheless still involves palatal lift. These directives establish the palatal lift, laryngeal settling, and tongue fronting needed for a well-opened throat. Between the top and bottom of this sensation, there is very little feeling, since the oropharyngeal area should be rather passive. In that regard, some earlier pedagogues have described this as feeling "throatless," or as if the throat were "invisible." (Trimble, 2015)

Acoustic Checking of First Formant Tuning

Various kinds of sounds can be introduced into the vocal tract to check the tuning and tone color of the first formant. In general, pharyngeal shaping is dominant for tuning the first formant, such that, the lower the first formant, the more open and settled the throat. The degree of lowering of the first formant should be balanced with comfort and "naturalness" of formation, ideally being shaped with the help of expressive motivation that attends to palatal height as well, without any tongue depression or the false (tongue backing) sensation of space toward the back wall of the oropharynx. In addition to seeking to establish a sufficiently low "pitch" of the first formant, listening for a first formant-dominated vowel quality is also effective in preparing an open throat for subsequent voicing. Among the options of sounds one might introduce into the vocal tract in order to check the tuning of the first formant are: whispering with ingressive (inhalatory) or eggressive (exhalatory) air movement; gentle ingressive or eggressive glottal clicks; and suction noises introduced at the lips. Notice that these sounds are all created at a tube end (glottis or lips), not by a narrowing within the tube.

Whispering

Modified whispering works well. Whispering involves positioning the glottis in an /h/ posture with nearly adducted vocal folds, followed by moving air through this position. The narrowed glottal slit will generate a range of frequencies that reveal the tuning of the lower formants. In instinctive whispering, the larynx is typically raised and the throat narrowed to emphasize the higher frequency tone color of the second formant, which is more essential to the definition and identity of most vowels. In order to use whispering to study the tuning of the first formant, care must be taken instead to produce open throated, low-pitched whispering with an appropriately settled larynx. This atypical style of whispering may sound somewhat "sketchy" as in naughty mischief but is excellent for working on lowering the pitch and vowel quality of the first formant while still attending to the higher partials being played by the second formant. Low pitched whispering—especially if done through a smile—still includes enough high frequencies to achieve a mixture of first and second formant influences in the composite sound, but will also be dominated enough by the first formant to reveal a perceptual vowel modification. The singer should neither form the speech level shape of the perceived modification nor collapse into a neutral vowel shape, but should deliberately maintain both the oral and pharyngeal shape of the intended vowel even though the resultant sound will migrate. For example, a well shaped /a/, when activated by a low-pitched, smiling whisper will sound rather modified toward /ʌ/. The singer should not collapse or change the /a/ shape to the speech shape of an /ʌ/, but should rather keep the shaping of the front room and ceiling of the mouth in that of a clear, bright /a/ even while hearing more of an /ʌ/. The /ʌ/-like timbre of the noise is due to the dominance of the pharyngeally tuned first formant. With practice the singer may be able to isolate the pitches and vowel qualities of both formants (over and under vowels) from the whisper and hear their contributions both individually and simultaneously, creating a kind of *chiaroscuro* whisper.

Glottal Clicks

Glottal clicks give a more sharply defined frequency cluster with which to ascertain formant tuning (a glottal click is accomplished by closing the glottis, preferably without laryngeal elevation, and then executing a short, clear, voiceless, low pressured glottal plosive, either ingressively or egressively). Throat opening, ingressive glottal clicks tend also to assist finding the lowest comfortable tuning of the first formant. Again it is helpful simultaneously to attend to an expressive lift of the palate rather than focusing only on laryngeal settling in order to avoid depressed or exaggerated lowering of the larynx. As described earlier, ingressive glottal suction is effective in stretching the thyrohyoid space and finding maximal throat openness. Following a glottal suction with a gentle ingressive glottal click can be very effective in counteracting habitually high laryngeal posturing. The clearer, more gently and briefly the glottal click is done, the better. Alternating and comparing ingressive and eggressive glottal clicks can help the singer establish a stable open throated vocal tract.

"Finger" Breathing

Inhaling while partially blocking the mouth with some part of the finger or hand can generate sufficient noise at the lips to play the resonance characteristics of the vocal tract (Arnold Jacob, Keith Underwood). In general, the louder and lower the "pitch" of the noise generated, the more open the throat. If the hand or finger is quickly removed mid-inhalation, the brief continuation of the inhalation will be noiseless if the throat is well opened. A disadvantage of this approach is the necessity to lip round against the hand/finger to assist in the noise generation, regardless of the vowel being tested. It is therefore most compatible with lip rounded vowels such as the vowel /ʊ/.

Comparison of Oral and Pharyngeal Dominance

It can be very clarifying kinesthetically to compare the sounds and sensations of any of these formant-checking noises (whisper, glottal click, finger breathing) when done with a relaxed larynx (an open throat and pharyngeal dominance) with that of a raised larynx (a closed throat and oral dominance). This is perhaps easiest to explore with whispering. Typical whispering is done with a raised larynx precisely in order to exaggerate the vowel differentiating, orally tuned second formant. For this exploration, the student must keep the palate and lips in the shape and look of, for example, an intended bright /a/ while alternating between both a typical, high-larynxed whisper and the low-pitched whisper suggested above. It helps to try to retain as much "brightness" of the over vowel as possible with the low-pitched whisper, to avoid the previously described false backspace percept of the lowered, backed up tongue bulge. The back of the tongue should remain released upward as the larynx and hyoid relax downward. In this comparison of low- and high-pitched whispering, the timbre of the resultant noise will alternate between /ʌ/ and /a/, and the student will notice the clear difference in throat posture. In a high pitched whisper, the resultant /a/-like noise comes from tuning the first formant, which should be contributing an /o/ to /ʌ/-like quality to the composite vowel timbre, to a higher frequency, so that its contribution instead reinforces the quality of the vowel defining mouth formant /a/. The difference between these postures can be augmented by motivating the exaggerated over vowel posture with a happier affect and egressive airflow or click, and the under vowel with an empathetic affect and ingressive flow or click.

This comparison also can be clearly revealed by closing the glottis and thumping the side of the larynx while alternating between the two throat postures. (This is easiest for those whose anatomy allows this trick, which is facilitated by having very little flesh or fat covering the larynx.) The error of raising the larynx to tune the first formant higher to increase second formant dominance and "help" define the target vowel is especially common on the open vowels, for which the first and second formants are already in closer proximity. That said, open vowels unfortunately do not have a monopoly on the innate larynx raising tendencies of singers in training. For a chart of the perceived tone color contributions of the first and second formants (also referred to in this text as pharynx/mouth; back room/front room; over vowel/under vowel), see Figure 6, p. 37.

Vowel Migrations at Harmonic: First Formant Intersections

When source harmonics approach and cross the first formant, there is an audible vowel migration created by passive modification. All harmonics other than the fundamental frequency of the sung pitch ($1f_o$) should be allowed to pass through the first formant without tracking, in other words, without shape change. The primary migration for (non-treble) male voices occurs at the first formant: second harmonic (F_1:$2f_o$) juncture an octave below the first formant, where the voice "turns over" from open timbre (*voce aperta*) to close timbre (*voce chiusa*). It occurs for treble voices at the first formant: *first* harmonic (F_1:$1f_o$) juncture, the transition into whoop timbre, where the sung pitch reaches the first formant. Anticipating and allowing these migrations at the very least, and even using strategies to facilitate them when necessary, is a key piece in training a throat to be consistently open across the singer's pitch range. This requires knowing where these migrations should occur by voice type and vowel, what the natural migrations will sound and feel like, and what thoughts or directives will assist in stimulating these responses. The pattern of first formant locations for cardinal vowels is easy to learn, consistent across voice types, and easily adjustable in pitch by voice type. The first formants of all other vowels can be reliably estimated from the cardinal vowel locations. Understanding and applying acoustic pedagogy requires that the teacher know approximate first formant locations. (See the chart of Approximate F_1 Locations by Voice under Pedagogic Resources at www.kenbozeman.com)

Migratory Paths by Vowel

As harmonics rise into and through the first formant, both the vowel and the vocal timbre will close somewhat. With the exception of /u/, the back vowels /ɑ ɔ ʊ o/ will move toward a closer neighbor. With the exception of /i/, the front vowels /æ ɛ e ɪ/ will both close and neutralize slightly. This is due to the fact that vowels modify toward the deepening quality of the first formant component, which usually features a harmonic with an absolute tone color of some form of /u/ or /o/. This merely closes the back vowels perceptually, since /u/ and /o/ also are members of the back vowel family. Therefore an /o/ migrates toward /u/, an /ɔ/ toward /o/ or /ʊ/, an /ɑ/ toward /ʌ/ or /ʊ/; however a passive migration of the front vowels—with an increasing /o/ or /u/ first formant component—both closes them and moves them toward the rounded, back vowel "side of the street" perceptually. This means that an /æ/ migration closes toward /ɛ/ and rounds toward /œ/; an /ɛ/ migrates toward /e/ or /ɪ/ with some /œ/; an /e/ toward /ɪ/ or /i/ with some /ø/, etc. There needn't be any front room assistance with this migration, that is, no "umlauted" lip rounding of the mouth shape. It is a passive modification that ideally occurs by changing the pitch with no change or compromise of the vocal tract shape, either of mouth or of open throat. Some successful singers and teachers use active modification of the front room (via lip rounding) to assist what can be a passive modification. Accomplishing it entirely with passive modification (that is, without shape change) gives greater awareness and control of the open throat posture and also better intelligibility by reducing both the appearance and degree of perceived modification. Remember, the front room is ideally about brightness, clarity, and vowel identity, and not for darkening or coloring the timbre (see Figure 6).

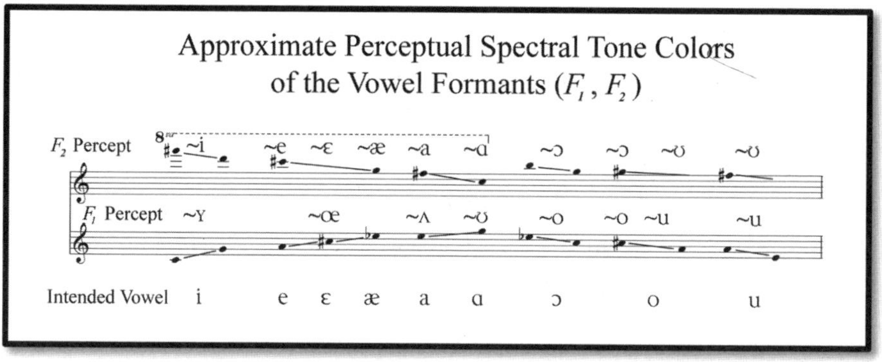

Figure 6: Perceptual Under (F_1) and Over (F_2) Vowel Modules

The Special Case of /i/ and /u/

Being the closest vowels, /i/ and /u/ have very low first formants, on or just below the bottom of the treble clef. They have no closer neighbor to which they could modify upon ascent. Most (though not all) singers allow /i/ and /u/ to transition to close timbre (non-treble voices singing pitches in the bass clef) or whoop timbre (treble voices singing pitches near the bottom of the treble clef) rather naturally and appropriately low in their respective ranges. These vowels therefore begin to need opening where other vowels are still close or closing. Given their low first formants, /i/ and /u/ are favorable for whooping but less compatible with yelling, hence there is somewhat less tendency to shorten the tube and open the mouth upon ascent. However, some singers will persist in staying in open timbre (non-treble male voices) when ascending, or inappropriately extend close timbre where whoop is appropriate (treble voices) on these two vowels by opening the vowel excessively and raising the larynx. Strategies must be used that maintain a settled, open laryngopharynx, keep the tongue dorsum high and the opening into the "front room" narrow. An ingressive, inhaled /k/ or German /ç/ followed by a low-pitched whispered /i/ and a back (rather than front) room vowel formation orientation can help position the tongue. Onsetting on an open-mouthed /ŋ/ followed by /i/ can orient the tongue dorsum height. Finally, imagining or actually inserting within a sustained, deep /i/ a series of rapidly articulated /j/ glides (/jijijijiji/) can help the singer find appropriate tongue dorsum height. If subtly done, this is hardly noticed, but succeeds in keeping the tongue bulge sufficiently close to the hard palate and the resultant /i/ sufficiently close. The physical positioning that assures the closure of the /i/ is to maintain back room depth and openness and a sufficiently narrow threshold into the front room through a high tongue hump (dorsum) and small slit between the tongue and hard palate. For /u/, inserting the /j/ glide in rapid succession (/jujujujuju/) will reduce excessive jaw drop and keep more high harmonic strength (ring) in the /u/.

Active Modification of /i/ and /u/

Knowing how to open the mouth for an /i/ in order to track the sung pitch with the first formant will take some exploration. The necessary objectives are to keep the oral shape of the "over vowel" deliberately well-tuned (a relaxed yet high tongue bulge close to the palate), while lowering the jaw to raise the first formant and increase the "under vowel" component. A strategy that takes advantage of instinct is to do a spontaneously motivated whoop glissando on /i/, or a celebratory, high-pitched, whooped "Yee-haw!" Many students will instinctively find a natural opening of the /i/ with such an exploration. In body mapping terms, as the jaw opens vertically, the hump of the tongue dorsum needs to stay high, close to the roof of the mouth, in contact with the side upper molars. An upper range /i/ will seem more centrally located in the mouth, rather than at the front teeth. Some use of affect to retain a high position of the "upper vowel" tuning is needed, even as the singer is concentrating more on the quality of the "under vowel" component. It may seem to the singer as if she is singing, at least in part, "behind and below" the tongue, "through the tongue," even "under the jaw" by the top of the treble clef, in order to keep the throat open and larynx settled. This does not result in vowel distortion, rather yields a fuller, yet still clear tone with good vowel identity. Non-treble male voices need to open the close vowels /i/ and /u/ through the male *zona di passaggio* in order to avoid or postpone arrival into whoop timbre. Treble voices need to open /i/ and /u/ starting by about G4 and A4 respectively.

Though it is counterintuitive given their close speech level shapes, pitches in the upper voice require that the jaw be more opened for /i/ and /u/ than for /ɑ/ in order to match /ɑ/ in overall timbre and resonance. As the jaw and mouth open more for an ascending /u/, the tongue bulge will need to float a bit higher in back, causing a low pitched whisper or glottal click to migrate to /ʊ/. The tongue tip can stay at the lower front teeth for most of the range, but depending upon individual morphology, may lose contact when the mouth is maximally opened. In that case, as the tongue tip loses that contact, it should at least be released toward the lower teeth rather than being actively retracted.

The More Open Vowels

All other, more open vowels frequently get caught up in the yell instinct with rising pitch, in which the first formant latches onto the harmonic rising through it and tracks it. Opening the mouth to formant track is appropriate for treble voices tracking whoop timbre (F_1:$1f_0$), but inappropriate for non-treble voices tracking a yell coupling (F_1:$2f_0$) above the normal turning, closing location of the vowel being sung, at least in Western classical technique. Both non-treble and treble voices need to stay in close articulation until the timbre closes or reaches whoop coupling, allowing the migration into a closer vowel through that transition. Non-treble male voices may either stay in close articulation above the turn, or—within a *voce chiusa* timbre—open the mouth some, retuning the over vowel, in order to find a second formant coupling with a higher harmonic (usually F_2:$3f_0$ or F_2:$4f_0$). After maximal vowel migration is reached at whoop coupling, treble voices will need to open all vowels above the pitch of coupling in order to track whoop timbre for higher pitches. Vowels other than /i/ and /u/ reach whoop coupling between about C5 and F#5. The vowel /ɑ/ only *has* to be opened starting at the top of the treble clef. Though this author recommends moderately close vowel articulation within the octave of close timbre (between turning over and whoop), one does have options there (such as opening the mouth more), as long as the back room is tall and well maintained (settled larynx, lifted palate).

Maintaining Tube Length and Shape

When passive vowel modification is all that is needed for a given situation, the task for the singer involves maintaining the vocal tract shape while changing the pitch. Learning how to maintain the shape of the vocal tract—the tube length (settled, open throat) and a close vowel posture—as a vowel migrates upon ascent is more challenging than one might think. This is most likely due to the fact that vowels are motivated more by means of the intended target vowel sound than by means of the kinesthetic sense of the vocal tract shape itself. As the vowel threatens to migrate, the singer instinctively changes the vocal tract in an attempt to avoid the migration and to retain the target vowel sound. Adding to the challenge is the fact that with changing pitch, the accompanying acoustic sensations also change (see Chapter 5). Furthermore, even when genuinely attempting to maintain length and closeness, beginners tend only to be able to manage one or the other (tube length or articulation closeness) but not both, or to lose track of the clarity of the vowel shape as the vowel migrates. What is needed is a motivation that sufficiently stabilizes the vocal tract shape for a given vowel without rigidity or interference. Many of the various kinesthetic suggestions of this text (better mapping of the throat and tongue, the two-room metaphor, descriptions of sound and sensation migrations, smile affect, etc.) are an attempt at gaining better control of vocal tract shaping to that end.

Pharyngeal Awareness

A counter-intuitive idea from early Italian pedagogy that can be very effective in maintaining tube shape and achieving a *chiaroscuro* balance is the assertion that vowels are formed low in the throat (pharynx) rather than primarily in the mouth (Lamperti) or that the real mouth for singing is the pharynx (Garcia, Bloem-Hubatka). The notion of forming vowels in the pharynx invites a legitimate concern that the resultant sound and production will be swallowed and throaty. However, when combined with the Italian directive to inhale through a smile, quite the opposite results. These complementary concepts counterbalance each other. The result is a complete vowel timbre that is seated deeper in the vocal tract, grounded in the body, and yet easy, clear, and even "sparkling," though a bit distant, as if "down the hall" or "down the tube" rather than mouthy.

The idea of clarity plus ease of throat prevents this from being actually throaty or swallowed in sound or sensation, and tends to preserve both adequate pharyngeal and oral shaping, while indirectly allowing migration. By contrast, a mouthy concept and orientation of vowel formation is likely to invoke a yell (or whisper) response in the attempt to avoid migration and result in an elevated larynx and shallow "white" timbre.

A related, equally counterintuitive directive that can assist in keeping the throat open and larynx settled is to imagine that the perceived ring of the vowel descends behind the tongue and down the throat as the pitch ascends, instead of climbing over the tongue and out of the front of the mouth, which would tend to raise the larynx and narrow the throat. This is similar to the more familiar pedagogic directive to think "down and in" as pitch ascends. It is also analogous to the bottom half of the epsilon image described below (p. 48).

Enunciation Orientation

Vowel clarity and identity are determined for most vowels by the tuning of the second formant, which is the formant that is most influenced by the tuning of the oral space in front of the tongue bulge that divides the vocal tract into two rooms. There is therefore a strong tendency for many students to orient their pronunciation as if centered in the mouth, or front room, rather than centering in the back room, nearer the actual center of the head and neck. This is the error of "going into the front room" with one's personal sense of agency. Pronouncing the vowels as if from the back room through the front room, while keeping the back wall appropriately fronted in sensation to avoid tongue backing and dulling of timbre, assists with depth of timbre and with the retention of a settled larynx and lifted palate. This approach is similar to the above-mentioned Italian *bel canto* directive to form the vowels in the pharynx.

Two Component Vowel Percept

In concert with the two-room metaphor and perception, with training, a student can hear and feel the individuality of the two vowel components: the deeper, pharyngeal, first formant component behind and below the tongue bulge; and the brighter, oral, clarity-inducing second formant component above, both at the top of the back room and, for lip rounded vowels, in front of the tongue bulge along the hard palate. As mentioned above, these can be identified as the "under vowel" and the "over vowel" components respectively. The over vowel component gives clarity and identity to the vowel, and should always be well-shaped both by the lifted soft palate, appropriate articulation in the front of the mouth, and even the subtle lift of light facial expression, rather than giving in to a lax, collapsed ceiling and deadpan expression. However, the sound of the over vowel is most apparent and prominent to the singer in the lower middle voice. Imbalanced exaggeration of the brighter over vowel component will result in a mouthy, shallow timbre and a tendency to have a one component, one room, mouth-dominated percept. The under vowel component, as the warming, rounding, and modifying element, should always be present in shape, and should increase in sound in the singer's perception with pitch ascent. Exaggeration of the rounding under vowel, if not complemented by the clarifying over vowel, will result in less distinct, less well differentiated vowels, a lower sensation of tonal "placement" and possibly a more effortful production. These two above and below components are best done not as an either/or, but in a both/and tandem. The under vowel component must seem independent of the tongue, that is, without depressing the back of the tongue. Rather, it is kinesthetically sensed as being accomplished below the tongue and jaw.

The Effect of Affect on the Over and Under Vowels

Both pleasurable and empathetic affects assist with the over and under vowel poise of the pharynx. However, pleasurable affects (smile, joy, mischief) tend to encourage the ringier timbre of the over vowel more, while pathetic (empathy, sympathy) or tender affects (love, sweetness) tend to encourage the warmer timbre of the under vowel more. One exception might be suppressed laugh, which has been shown to retract the false vocal folds (Estill), and which therefore would lower and increase the first formant contribution. Warmer affects also seem to correlate and coordinate well with the in, down, and out breath management strategies that encourage some inhalatory resistance to compression of the torso, so necessary to pressure reduction during singing.

The Vertical Alignment of the Over and Under Vowel Percepts

Though there is usually a frontal acoustic sensation component to resonant vowels, it is very helpful to sense a more central, vertical alignment of the over and under vowels. The over vowel is directly above the under vowel sensation. They are not to be aligned horizontally in the front and back of the mouth, giving that false sense in increased length from the lips to the back of the throat. Their vertical alignment is especially helpful when ascending into the upper range, where there can be a strong, misguided tendency to increase the front to back horizontal length percept. Increasing the front to back percept accompanies a lowering and backing of the back of the tongue into the pharynx, a rising larynx, a loss of vertical alignment, and a reduction in vertical length. The singer should avoid compressing the back of the tongue and the hyoid bone together. That is, the singer should avoid activating the hyoglossus and styloglossus muscles, whose contractions reduce the independence of tongue and larynx. Perception of front to back length is contrary to perception of top to bottom length/tallness; increasing one decreases the other. Maintaining and even stretching the sense of vertical length and alignment of the two components, while keeping the front to back dimension short (keeping the back wall sensation fronted), keeps the larynx settled, the throat opened, the tongue bulge high, the tongue root loose, and the resonator convergent.

Chiaroscuro Reconsidered

The Italian school concept of *chiaroscuro* is usually understood to mean a bold juxtaposition and balance of bright and dark timbral elements. In the visual arts, these components are kept in somewhat stark contrast to create a sense of dimension. This remains a helpful analogy for Western classical vocal timbre. A balance of depth and brilliance is characteristic of classical tone, and the singer should strive to maximize and juxtapose both aspects rather than seeking a compromised, blended middle ground. When properly conceived and executed, increasing one increases the other in a healthy, pleasing balance. When falsely conceived they operate in opposition, such that increasing one reduces the other. Asking the student to darken or brighten the tone tends to invoke this false opposition of mouth and pharynx rather than the mutually helpful, cooperative balance of a *chiaroscuro* combination. (see Composition of the Tonal Sensation: Ring vs. Color below, p. 50).

A useful alternative understanding of the *chiaroscuro* concept, rather than as an adjective-adjective designation, is as an adjective-noun combination describing a specific kind of depth or darkness: a ringing depth or a brilliant darkness. The depth component—which might be considered the foundational core of a healthy technique, since it is due to an appropriately opened throat—should have a clarion quality. This way of conceiving timbral depth helps the singer avoid the dull, fuzzy, woofy, or throaty effect of wrongly conceived depth. For example, attempting a round, close /o/ "under vowel" that is perceived to be formed in the laryngopharynx below the tongue can assist freedom and efficiency of phonation, as long as the tongue dorsum is high and the singer doesn't depress the larynx or "dig" for the sense of depth. Conceiving that deeply formed /o/ as ringing, clear, and "sparkling" counteracts the tendency to depress the larynx, as does a slightly elevated rather than tucked head posture.

Lip Rounding vs. Lip Spreading

Excellent singers and teachers can be found that use some degree either of facial lift and smile or, conversely, of lip relaxation, rounding, or even protruding. Lip spreading is cited by the latter group as inducing a narrowing of the throat, raising of the larynx, and "spreading" of the tone. A coupling of the smile with a narrowed throat can indeed be an instinctive co-present behavior for some, especially if the smile is conceived as mainly external and facial, but such coupling is not an inevitable, necessary response. It is true that lip spreading alone has the acoustic effect of slightly shortening vocal tract length, which effect would raise all formants a bit and brighten the overall timbre. However, as reported earlier, historic Italian *bel canto* pedagogy recommended inhaling through a smile to open the throat. A "pharyngeal" smile that is internally motivated (from the inside out rather than the outside in) is more likely to open the throat, lower the larynx, and raise the palate. Smiling from a "front room," mouthy orientation would surely raise the larynx, narrow the throat, and make the timbre shallow and spread.

Conversely, lip rounding is a frequently encountered pedagogic strategy. It might in fact induce a settling of the larynx for some, but probably does not induce a lifted palate. Lip rounding and lip protruding lengthen the vocal tract, lowering all formants and warming or deepening the overall timbre. Lip "trumpeting" (protruding) is sometimes seen in low male singers attempting to deepen their timbre, if not their vocal *Fach* beyond their natural physiology. Poorly executed, it can dull the timbre, create an artificial degree of depth or maturity, and distort or muddle diction.

It apparently is possible to retrain either of these coupled responses to good effect, since successful singers can be found on either side of this issue. This author prefers to train for throat-opening pre-phonatory tuning in concert with moderate expressive affect and articulation largely modeled after speech. This is in alignment with historic Italian *bel canto* pedagogy, with its pleasantly expressive smile imagery and "*si canta come si parla*" orientation. Any position one espouses can be misapplied or done to excess. Some students, with tongue and throat tightness tendencies, may respond better to a more passive facial use or the actively modified approach of frontal rounding. In the end, neither emotive mugging with excess facial tension, nor deadpan, expressionless droop is desirable. The Italian approach, when well executed, facilitates an appropriate degree of visual expression and clarity of diction within a balanced, *chiaroscuro* timbre. A relaxed, rounded mouth posture when coupled with sufficient inner height can also get good results. In short, if the "back room" is well formed with a settled larynx, open throat, lifted palate, and a released, fronted tongue, one has options for shaping the "front room."

Chapter 5
Sensation Migration Across Range

Qualification of Descriptions of Subjective Sensations

The acoustic sensation of a sung tone is comprised of various facets, resulting in part from it being composed of several formants, each of which create standing waves at different frequencies and therefore vibrational *foci* at various locations along the vocal tract. In addition to vocal tract sensations are those that result from considerable bone conduction of vibration in the head, neck and even in the chest wall. The singer's perception of tonal sensations will therefore be due in large measure to that facet to which her mind is attending. Sensitivity to vibratory sensations and bio-feedback also varies from singer to singer. These acoustic sensations change dynamically with change of pitch across the singer's range. Furthermore, they interact with the kinesthetic sensations of anatomic shape, position, or posture of the vocal tract. The complexity of these sensory signals necessitates flexibility, ongoing discussions with and feedback from the student, and avoidance of dogmatic insistence in the use of specific "placement" or other sensory imagery. Nonetheless, there are general patterns of perceived sensation relative to range that are common enough to prove helpful.

Degrees of Openness and Closure

As explained earlier, the same vocal tract and mouth shape will yield increasingly closer vowels and timbre with pitch ascent, and increasingly open vowels and timbre with pitch descent. This phenomenon necessitates developing the ability to differentiate sensations of shape from those of sound and of acoustic vibration. For situations in which passive vowel modification is recommended—most situations and registers below whoop coupling—shape must be maintained even while experiencing changes in timbre and in acoustic sensation. Aural migrations are accompanied by some change in acoustic sensation. Acoustic sensations cannot be "held" in place. Lower pitches with a more open timbre have a brassier quality and seem to ring more directly in the front of and out of the mouth. The closer timbres of higher pitches are smoother, "creamier," feel rounder, perhaps more domed, and somewhat more internalized. It can be helpful to think more "in and down" with higher pitches, and more frontal and on the hard palate and at the front teeth with low pitches.

The Epsilon Image

In the lower middle voice of (non-treble) male voices and the lower voice of treble voices, the sound may seem to ring rather directly out of the mouth. As pitch ascends, the sound sensation may either have a component that curves behind, up and over the soft palate into the front half of the head, or a component that settles and curves behind and below the tongue and jaw and into the body, or possibly both simultaneously. These paths approximately describe the shape of an epsilon (ε) or the number 3, depending upon one's orientation, which is open to the front with its curves to the back. With this image in mind, the singer's orientation is encouraged to be more vertical and aligned near the front of the back room (see the paragraphs on the two room analogy [p. 18] or vertical alignment [p. 43] explained earlier) rather than out in the front room and "mouthy" upon ascending. The yell instinct causes the untrained singer to lose the two-room sensation, to over open the mouth, and to lose inner depth with a raised larynx, narrowed pharynx, and divergently shaped vocal tract. The epsilon image helps maintain enough tongue height to create convergence, maintain throat openness and *chiaroscuro* timbre. Though this image is oriented and centered somewhat in (the front of) the back room, it will be important to keep the front room well-tuned for vowel clarity. When descending again into the lower voice, the tone can be felt to vibrate more into and out of the mouth, like the middle leg of the epsilon or three. (See Figure 7, p. 48)

The Capital C Image

When singing in the range of close or whoop timbre, that is, above open timbre, the epsilon-like acoustic sensation may simply seem more like a large capital C, rounded to the back and open to the front without the middle leg of the epsilon image. Its upper arch is above the level of the mouth, and its lower extension curves behind and below the tongue and jaw in perception. In general for *chiaroscuro* timbre the singer should seek more acoustic sensation above and/or below the mouth, rather than primarily or only in the mouth.

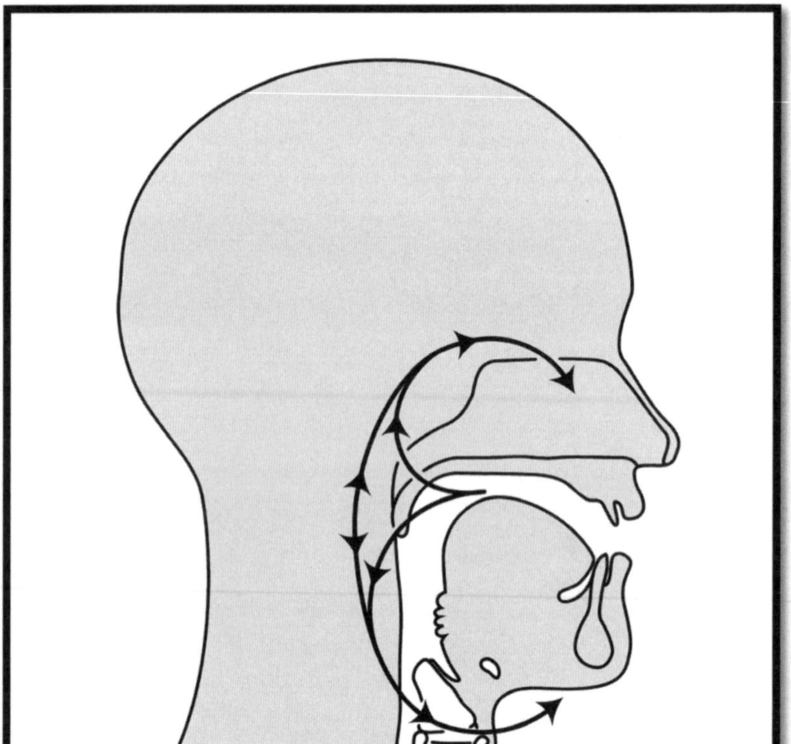

Figure 7: Epsilon and Capital C Images for Sensation of Acoustic Migration across Range

Caveat

These two images are not intended to be prescriptive of acoustic sensation. For example, treble voices singing in their upper range may perceive vibratory sensations to be quite high in the head, and even as if outside the head, as if helmet-like in shape and location. With all sensory imagery, ongoing dialogue and confirmation with the individual singer is necessary.

Sensation of Convergence

Singing with a convergent resonator shaping has different acoustic sensations from those of a divergent shaping. The sensation of the top of a convergent resonator, with a palate well raised by some appropriate affect (pharyngeal smile, empathy, etc.), creates awareness of height in the back room in front of the ears—approximately between the temporomandibular joints—that then angles downward toward the hard palate. Affective motivation must be kept strong across vowel and pitch changes to maintain palatal height with this angle of the ceiling percept of the vocal tract. The soft palate should not relax into a collapsed, drooping sensation. Furthermore, collapsing the palate tends to accompany a less settled larynx, moving the overall vocal tract shape toward divergence. This is especially true of the French nasal vowels, which should be accomplished by fronting the soft palate more than by simply lowering it. The singer will find that in order for the vowel to rhyme with its unnasalized form (for example, /õ/ with /o/) she will need to shape for convergence more aggressively for the nasal version. Without special attention, nasalizing a vowel will shift it toward a more open version of the vowel. For example, nasalizing an /o/ will result in a shift in vowel quality to an /ɔ̃/, if the palate was lowered rather than fronted in order to add the nasalance. Furthermore, as the palate lowers, the glottis tends to rise, and possibly leak more air, reducing the depth and completeness of *chiaroscuro* timbre. Temporarily onsetting the nasal vowel with a gentle glottal stroke can help counteract and correct both a leaky glottis and droopy palate. Fronting the soft palate refers to achieving nasalization by pulling the back of the soft palate away from the back throat wall without relaxing and lowering it, that is, while deliberately attempting to keep the front of the soft palate lifted. It may feel as if one is trying to raise the back of the hard palate.

While the tongue should be mapped to remain as high and fronted as the vowel and pitch will allow, the "floor of the back room," which is at the base of the larynx behind and below the tongue and jaw, should be felt to stay low and with some lateral width. This sensation of the height and depth of the back room should be accomplished without adding the false sensation of space in the oropharynx, directly behind the mouth. The back wall of the oropharynx should be relaxed and mapped in order to be felt where it actually is: in front of the ears.

Composition of the Tonal Sensation: Ring vs. Color

Those coaching the interpretation of texted music often encourage the singer to find and access a wide variety of "colors" of tone, in order to have tones appropriate to a variety of situations and feelings. Although the communicative, artistic goal of this advice is laudable, there is danger in thinking in terms of "coloring" the voice. A well-resonated tone feels as if both its depth and brilliance are comprised entirely of ring, that is, of both low and high ringing frequencies, not so much of color, which thought instead risks reducing the energy of source harmonics and dulling or overly darkening the timbre. "Coloring" the voice is more likely to induce artificial manipulations of the vocal tract that are less speech-like. The safer way to achieve variety of color is to motivate the sound with a variety of genuine affects. Affects create subtle changes that are more functionally efficient, innate, and less likely to be formed manipulatively or to sound false or insincere. Sincere affective motivation plus the thought of making all of one's sounds out of "ring" sensations in both pharynx and mouth yield the most efficient, effective results.

Head Alignment

In general head posture should not need to be adjusted for vowel change or pitch change. A relatively level head posture can accommodate all vowels and most of the range. However, if the student is struggling with range or loading up too much vocal weight when ascending in pitch, a slight elevation of the head coupled with settling the "underbelly" of the tonal sensation into the torso can assist with freeing the upper range. To be clear, this is not a reaching up and forward of the chin, a move which typically accompanies laryngeal elevation; rather it is a settling back and up with good vertical alignment of head, neck and chest, and perhaps with a feeling of expressive warmth and of relaxation of the neck into the sternum area. It is important to maintain the inner palatal lift of an affective motivation as a complement to the settled larynx, as well as continued inhalatory checking of breath pressure. Taken together these strategies discourage heaviness. The alternative strategy—chin tucking—may add "color" or depth but also invites heaviness of vocal load.

Acoustic Sensations of Close Timbre

As described above, if vocal tract shape is maintained, vowels migrate closer with pitch ascent, and general timbre also migrates in a manner that was described by the Italian school as going from *aperta* (open) to *chiusa* (close). While the sensation of shape would stay the same, the acoustic sensations migrate in ways described above as well (see Epsilon Image, for example). The crucial move from open to close timbre at the $F_1{:}2f_0$ juncture is also perceived as accompanied by acoustic sensations for which the descriptive term *chiusa* is especially apt. The sound sensation becomes increasingly "gathered" or concentrated through the *zona di passaggio,* as if collecting into a singularity. This is certainly what Italian tenor, Luciano Pavarotti meant when he stated in public master classes that he wanted all young male singers (especially tenors) to "close" in the *passaggio*, instead of singing "open." Images and gestures that reinforce this migration of sensation can help the student close the timbre. While the actual vowel shape should not widen with ascent as it would in open, spread timbre, neither is the appropriately narrowed acoustic sensation achieved by any actual physical narrowing, compression, or inhibition in the vocal tract. Only those shaping factors that are achieving the convergence, such as the tongue bulge or the lip rounding, need to stay close in shaping sensation. Neither the back nor the front room should close or be reduced in size in order to close the timbre or vowel. In other words, the closing of the timbre is an acoustic sensation, which results from passive migration and does not require an actual physical reduction in shape or space.

Affective Migration

Since voicing is innately motivated by expression as previously asserted, both pitch and laryngeal registration are most directly accessed by means of an affective impulse. This can be used to assist with transitions across and through laryngeal registers. While a singer may need to be able to express a variety of emotions in all parts of the range, different affects more spontaneously stimulate different range areas, just as in expressive speech inflection. Experimenting with affective progressions that inspire pitch inflection across the entire compass of a voice is productive. For example, affects that assist in accessing lower register function include mild anger, mischief, or, for more lyric situations, reassurance. Affects that assist the transition to the lighter laryngeal adjustments needed for ascending include sweetness, empathy, or for more energetic situations, joy, celebration.

The Tongue, Larynx, and Back of the Throat

With pitch ascent and jaw lowering, there often also is an instinct to begin to lower the back of the tongue, the tongue dorsum, to create a sense of space. This is usually accompanied by the perception of greater distance from front to back, and loss of the downward angle of the "ceiling" of the back room. Like the sensation of backspace in the oropharynx, this is a false percept. The tongue should be released to float up and back perceptually as the jaw lowers in active vowel modification. The hyoid bone and larynx should simultaneously feel as if settling down in the opposite direction from the tongue dorsum. Paradoxically, when the tongue lowers, the larynx often rises. This can be due to the contraction of the hyoglossus muscles, those lateral muscle sheaths that rise from the side wings of the hyoid bone and insert into the back sides of the tongue. Remapping this so that the hyoglossus relaxes allows the tongue to release upward and the hyoid/larynx to release downward, creating more independence of tongue and hyoid/larynx unit. As the tongue dorsum "floats up" the larynx releases and settles. This helps to maintain tongue height, resonator convergence from glottis to tongue bulge, and accompanies the above-cited part of the acoustic sensation of singing increasingly behind and below the tongue, rather than over the tongue and out of the mouth.

Furthermore, if the perception of the back wall of the throat is kept forward in front of the ears, where it actually resides, while the tongue dorsum floats up and back, it may seem that the distance between the top of the tongue bulge and the back wall narrows. This sensation of front-to-back narrowness is actually evidence of an open throat, and encourages sensation of ring, both at the top of the pharynx between the temporomandibular joints as well as lower, near the glottis. Conversely, the false sensation of space in the back of the mouth from a lowered tongue dulls timbre. A sense of lateral space between the temporomandibular joints, along with a kind of double dome—one to either side—is helpful in maintaining a sufficiently high palate with some high partial (ringy) tonal sensations above the level of the mouth.

Laryngeal Position

It is instinctive for humans to raise the larynx with rising pitch and to lower the larynx for the lowest pitches of the range. This innate tendency must be largely countered in Western classical singing so that a relatively stable tube length prevails. Much of this text is concerned with addressing the former, more prevalent challenge—laryngeal elevation with ascending pitch. Strategies such as anticipating vowel migration and closure, increasing the percentage of the perceived under vowel, thinking directionally in, back, and down, behind and below the tongue, and warm, empathetic affects, for example, all discourage laryngeal elevation and encourage an open throat and an appropriate, general stability of tube length. However, when descending into the lowest register, singers may be inclined to tuck the chin and "dig" for sound with resultant laryngeal depression. Anticipating an opening and brightening of the tone, more vibratory feedback along the hard palate, vowel migration toward more open neighbors, and the sense that the sound is ringing more directly out of the mouth counteract this tendency and assist with lower voice freedom. It can also help to allow the larynx to seem to rise or actually rise a bit for the lowest pitches to assist with this brightness. At this point low in the singer's range, slight laryngeal elevation should not result in any forward, upward reaching of the head. These complementary directives—to think down and in for ascending pitch and more up and out for descending pitch—are not new to voice pedagogy. The use of a pleasurable affect to motivate this brightening of lower tones, increased awareness of ring in the area of the nasopharynx, or a moderating description such as, "Allow the larynx to 'float up' a little for better ring on low notes," helps to avoid any actual pressed phonation. Furthermore, just as the singer should anticipate and perceive an increasing percentage of the under vowel component with ascending pitch, an increasing percentage of the over vowel component—to the point of exclusive perception of the over vowel—should accompany the lowest tones of the range.

Mouth Shape

The subject of preferred mouth shape for singing was begun earlier (Lip rounding vs. Lip spreading, p. 44). The early Italian *bel canto* preference for a pleasant expression, with at least the hint of a smile, has much in its favor. The mouth when closed is, after all, a horizontal slot. When it opens in a relaxed manner, it retains a horizontal oval shape through normal jaw rotation, even more so when accompanied by light expression, which activates slight lift of the cheeks. Most speech articulation retains this general shape, and even those vowels that round the lips rarely take the shape as far as a vertical oval within speech range. Both rejoicing and lamenting tend to find expression through more or less lateral oval to possibly round shapes with some activation of cheek muscles. Only with significant jaw translation and active lip rounding—both of which necessitate more deliberate muscular action—are vertical oval mouth shapes achieved. While this preponderance of neutral lateralness at the lips is natural, neither the sensations of the internal vocal tract shape, nor the acoustic sensations accompanying singing need be predominantly lateral. The vocal tract is a curved vertical tube. The acoustic sensations in successfully resonated sounds in Western classical style are felt to be more vertical than lateral, and increasingly so with ascending pitch. Furthermore these acoustic sensations are not confined to the oral cavity, rather they extend above and below the mouth.

Top/Bottom vs. Front/Back Percept

The perception of increase in the length of the top to bottom dimension (palate to glottis) of the tonal sensation is inversely related to the perception of front to back length (lips to throat wall). A taller top to bottom percept means a shorter front to back percept. Greater front to back length reduces top to bottom height and actually backs the tongue into the pharynx. The singer should arrange perception to maximize the top to bottom height perception and minimize front to back length perception. Too much awareness of the throat wall directly behind the mouth can cause a sense of lengthening the front/back dimension, again backing the tongue into the lower pharynx. When tongue lowering (hyoglossus) and tongue retracting (styloglossus) muscles are relaxed and released, the student will not have much sensation directly in back other than that of muscular freedom. Instead, there may be more awareness of vertical space or lift above the level of the mouth in the nasopharynx (roughly between the temporomandibular joints) and settling and relaxing below the tongue and jaw at the laryngeal level or lower neck.

Nasopharyngeal Function and Sensation

In successful *chiaroscuro* timbre, there can be a strong awareness of vibration or ring in the vicinity of the nasopharynx, at the top of the "back room." There is ongoing debate and research on whether or not this is due to standing waves in the vocal tract or actual nasalance (separation of the soft palate and throat wall, allowing some airflow into and through the nose). There are studies that suggest both answers to this question (Perna: 2008, 2014; Austin: 1997, 2000; Sundberg: 2007). What so far has been agreed upon is that no one is suggesting the desirability of a high percentage of nasalance with a resultant percept of nasality for the audience. Historic *bel canto* pedagogy has generally assumed and maintained the goal of complete closure of the nasal port. After all, the nasal cavity is not an effective resonator, tending instead to reduce the intensity of higher partials. There may however be other benefits to slight nasalance. Future studies will have to resolve this question definitively. Whether or not there is actual nasalance, a more relevant study would investigate the usefulness of deliberate nasalance in training singers. Meanwhile, the existence of perceptual vibration or ring in the vicinity of the nasopharynx can be shared by both sides of this debate. It may also be the case that the uvula and back edge of the soft palate is active in tuning the vocal tract with or without allowing actual opening into the nasal port and true nasalance. On the one hand, the sensation of the kind of palatal lift that accompanies the dull-timbred, hyponasal characature of stuffy-nosed speech is not desireable. Notice the kinship between this aural effect and sensation with that of the tongue-backing, front to back lengthening percept. On the other hand, it is possible to have strong nasopharygeal ring sensation with little to no air escaping the nares, i.e., minimal to no nasalance.

The nasopharyngeal area is preferable to the front of the mouth for much of the range for sensing the *chiaro* aspect of a balanced timbre. Sensation of nasopharyngeal ring supports a vertical, two-component, above and below percept of vowel and tone in contrast to a horizontal, one room, mouthy percept. It is also compatible with the Italian *bel canto* advice to form the vowels (at least perceptually) in the pharynx. In this regard, conceiving the *chiaroscuro* components of a vowel as being formed, or at least as being primarily located in the laryngopharynx (under vowel) and nasopharynx (over vowel), while avoiding excessive oropharyngeal sensation yields the best result. Oropharygeal sensation tends to induce tongue backing and timbral dulling.

Chapter 6

Comparison of Treble and Non-Treble Voice Training

Comparative Questions

Young teachers rightly wonder about the similarities and differences between the training of non-treble (bass, baritone, tenor) and treble (countertenor, alto, mezzo, soprano) voices, especially in the areas of laryngeal registration and acoustic registration. For example, are the issues and strategies the same, only an octave displaced? Or are they more or less the same at approximately the same pitches?

Similarities

Certainly many basic matters of voice training are very nearly the same. Physical alignment of the torso and head is generally the same for all singers. Differences in balance may have more to do with body type and weight than with physical sex. The same could be said for breathing—generally the same approach applies to all, adapted perhaps a bit for height and weight. Both male and female voices have essentially the same laryngeal register options: primarily being mode one (M1, historic chest register) with a shorter, thicker vocal fold shape and mode two (M2, historic head register) with a longer, thinner vocal fold shape. Transitioning from M1 to M2 and back can and should be trained in all voices, with the goal of negotiating this shift as smoothly as possible. Downstream resisters and semi-occluded vocal tract articulations are very useful in pursuing this objective. This shift can occur at nearly the same pitch for male and female voices—somewhere between C4 and G4, usually close to E4. In this regard, male laryngeal registration can be exercised and trained like female laryngeal registration and vice-versa. In Western classical timbre, non-treble males do not resort to M2 very often in literature, except for high quiet floating effects or buffo effects, but it is good to explore this transition nonetheless for ease of laryngeal registration. Treble voices however do cross over into M1 for power and projection on their lowest tones, while singing most of their range in M2.

Differences

Differences in laryngeal register and acoustic register have to do with differences in anatomy and physiology. Male larynxes post puberty experience a significant growth spurt that makes them both larger and more angular in front. Female larynxes are on average 60-70 percent as large as male larynxes and more rounded in front. Female vocal folds are approximately 70-80 percent as long as male vocal folds, and adult female vocal tracts are ca. 80 percent as long as adult male vocal tracts. These size differences result in female ranges being about one octave higher than male ranges, but female resonances (vocal tract formants) average being only about a major third higher than the average male formants. There is as much or more difference between male vocal tract lengths (from basses to *leggiero* tenors) than between the average of male and female vocal tract lengths. The main and most crucial implication of these physiologic differences is that though treble voice range is an octave higher than non-treble range, female resonances are only a step or two higher than male resonances. This results in significant necessary differences in acoustic circumstance and strategy. Treble voices at an octave higher than non-treble voices have half as many harmonics within primary timbral range (roughly that of the piano keyboard) with which to construct their tones. With shorter vocal tracts, female voices also have fewer formants within the keyboard with which to resonate those fewer available harmonics.

Acoustic Differences

Non-treble ranges are between ca. C2 (basses) and C5 (tenors), and mostly between ca. G2 and A4, that is, mostly below the treble clef. Treble voice ranges are typically between about F3 (mezzos) and Eb6 (coloraturas), but mostly between ca. A3 and B-flat 5, through and above the treble clef. Since almost all first formants of all voice types lie in contact with the treble clef, the sung pitches of non-treble voices only occasionally intersect a few of these formants. Treble voices, on the other hand, frequently sing pitches that cross all of their vowels' first formants. Non-treble voices therefore are most often singing in open timbre (more than an octave below F_1) or close timbre (within an octave below F_1), but rarely in whoop timbre (at or above F_1). Treble voices are singing in close timbre (within an octave below F_1) or whoop timbre (at or above F_1), but rarely in open timbre (more than an octave below F_1). (See Figure 8.) Treble voices can and do experience open timbre and laryngeal mode one for open vowels on pitches sung below the bass clef notes in Figure 8, and can be trained similarly to male *passaggio* in this range to good effect for a smoother transition from mode one to mode two.

Figure 8. Approximate Acoustic Events for a Soprano

Furthermore, lower male range can involve the intersection of harmonics higher than the second ($2f_0$) with the first formant, generating timbral closures other than the primary $2f_0$ crossing of F_1, from open to close timbre. (See Figure 9.) Some of these "mini-turnings" are crucial for traversing the male *zona di passaggio.* For example, the crossing of the 3rd harmonic ($3f_0$) above the first formant of the open vowels /ɛ/, /ɑ/, and /ɔ/ (indicated by the dark gray notes in Figure 9) helps to define the *primo passaggio* or entry into the *zona di passaggio.* If these mini-closures do not happen, the male singer will have raised his larynx and will be singing too "wide open" already through the *zona di passaggio,* making the transition through the *secondo passaggio* into the upper voice even more difficult.

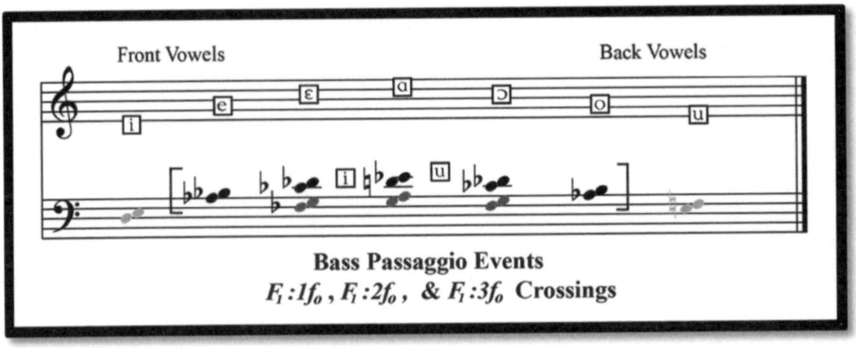

Figure 9. Acoustic Events of the Male *Zona di Passaggio*

Other "mini-closures" or "mini-openings" below the *passaggio* also can be observed. As the male sings more than two octaves below a vowel formant, the timbre and vowel open even further as the 4th harmonic ($4f_o$) drops below the first formant. In that situation the shape of the vowel may need to be closed a bit with some vowels in order to meet the expectations of diction. Ascending through these same pitches will result in closures of timbre and vowel.

These lower "mini-closures," which occur when harmonics three or four cross the first formant, sufficiently mimic in sound and sensation the more primary migrations of the first and second harmonics to be of pedagogic use. They can be used by teacher or student for modeling vowel migration sensations at pitches less encumbered with the laryngeal registration issues of higher closures, especially for male voices. This phenomenon also allows repeated teacher modeling at comfortable pitches and low breath pressure levels through the course of a long teaching day. Predicting these closure locations is as simple as knowing the first formant locations of seven cardinal vowels (Figures 8 or 9) and the intervals between the the sung pitch (the fundamental frequency) and the 2nd, 3rd, and 4th harmonics: an octave; an octave and a fifth; two octaves.

Differing Acoustic Strategies

Sounds of the passive vowel migrations that occur when turning over from open to close timbre (when the second harmonic ($2f_o$) approaches the first formant (F_1) in male voices) and when moving into whoop timbre (when the first harmonic, i.e., the sung pitch ($1f_0$) approaches the first formant (F_1) in treble voices) are indeed similar and in relatively similar locations within their respective ranges. For example, an /o/ goes from open to close timbre, or "turns over" in a high baritone range at about B3-C4. The same /o/ arrives in whoop timbre in a treble voice an octave higher at about C5. The closure of timbre for the former is quite similar to the maximal migration achieved at whoop timbre of the latter that octave higher. This phenomenon is replicated for every vowel an octave apart between treble and non-treble voices. This similarity of acoustic migration events between the male and female upper middle voices may have led some to assume that their acoustic registration issues are the same. While both should stay in close articulatory shaping when entering that migration, their strategies must differ *above* those events. Males can stay in close articulation for some time above the turn. Females should begin opening the vowel above arrival in whoop in order to track whoop timbre higher, or their vocal quality will thin. Therefore treble voices face the need to actively modify vowels by opening them relatively earlier in their ranges, while non-treble males do not necessarily have to open vowel articulations except for the few vowels whose first formants are within their range (/i/ /y/and /u/). Furthermore, treble voices do not face the "mini-turns" or "mini-closures" a P5th below whoop coupling that the non-treble males face a P5th below their primary turn, nearer to their *primo passaggio.* The next lower event below whoop timbre in the female voice is a full octave lower, where $2f_0$ crosses F_1, going from open to close timbre. Treble voices usually only experience that event on their most open vowels in their lower range in pitches at and below the treble clef.

Differing Acoustic Sensations

It must be pointed out that given the different octaves in which treble and non-treble singers sing, and the corresponding differences in harmonic: formant interactions, acoustic sensations and perceptions will also differ to some extent. For example, the higher one sings, the more centralized sensations of vowel vibratory locus ("placement?") may seem. While there are parallels between male and female "placement" perceptions, there are also real differences that must be respected. And in all cases, given the variety of perceptions even within the same voice type, student feedback should be sought and dogmatic insistence on specific vibratory feedback perceptions avoided.

Summary

In Western classical technique, non-treble voices (basses, baritones and tenors):

- sing almost exclusively in laryngeal mode 1 (historic chest)
- sing in open and close timbre, but only rarely in whoop
- rely primarily on passive vowel migration (maintaining vocal tract shape while the vowel migrates with pitch change)
- must use active vowel modification (opening) on their closest vowels into and above the *zona di passaggio* in order to avoid whoop coupling and to retain virile timbre
- may use active vowel modification (opening, tongue shaping) in order to find a coupling between the second formant and the 3rd or 4th harmonic for a more ringing, robust top tone

In Western classical technique, treble voices (altos, mezzos, countertenors and sopranos):

- sing in both laryngeal modes 1 and 2, though more often in mode 2 (historic head)
- sing in close and whoop timbre, but only rarely in open
- rely on both passive migration (below whoop) and active modification (from whoop on up)
- must use active vowel modification (opening) on all vowels above their first formant locations for full resonance with warmth and roundness
- tune the vocal tract so that the first harmonic ($1f_0$) dominates the timbre from about D5 on up for fullness of timbre. This involves tracking the sung pitch with the first formant, but may also involve "detuning" the second formant away from higher harmonics (via tongue shape changes) to avoid shrillness.
- alternatively, may stay in close vowel postures above first formant locations, if seeking a soft, silvery float timbre (a strategy that would be shrill if sung at higher intensities)

Chapter 7
Belting Revisited

Caveat

As reported in *Practical Vocal Acoustics*, I am trained and primarily experienced in teaching Western classical singing. I do venture occasionally into styles involving belting, but claim no special expertise in teaching belt. I am nonetheless often asked how one should apply the emerging knowledge of voice acoustics to other styles, especially those involving or related to belting. At the time of this publication, the acoustic characteristics of higher belt and "mix" strategies need further study by scientists collaborating with specialists in those vocal styles. I offer here tentative observations that may eventually either be verified or need adjusting by the results of future investigations.

The Variety of Pedagogic Approaches

There are currently a number of pedagogic training options spanning a variety of approaches to the teaching of belt, including Jo Estill; Seth Riggs and his successors (Speech Level Singing—SLS organizations: IVTOM, IVA); Jeannette LoVetri (Somatic Voicework); Lisa Popeil (Voiceworks); Mary Saunders-Barton (Bel canto can belto); and Robert Edwin, to name but a few prominent, successful teachers and approaches in the United States. There is also a growing list of specific kinds of belt, separated by genre, some of which may seem only discernable to or debated by belt specialists.

The Acoustics of Belting

From an acoustic point of view, belting attempts to extend a speech-like quality throughout the range and to mimic the powerful and dramatic effect of the yell for climactic emotional effect. As reported in *Practical Vocal Acoustics*, this is accomplished mostly on open vowels in that part of the range at which first formant tracking of the second harmonic of those vowels is possible (ca. D4-C5, a bit lower or higher depending on vowel and voice type). Physically, this involves the following: as the second harmonic approaches the frequency peak of the first formant, the vowel is increasingly opened, and for most methods, some degree of laryngeal elevation is allowed or actually employed (whether directly or indirectly motivated) to raise the first formant in tandem with the rising second harmonic, an octave above the sung pitch. Both of these maneuvers—as in whispering—reduce pharyngeal resonance and create a divergently shaped resonator with greater mouth dominance, and a more speech-like timbre throughout the range. In contrast to raw yelling, skilled belters must accomplish this at breath pressure and glottal resistance levels that are low enough to be sustainable and healthy, since these maneuvers invoke a higher degree of glottal resistance than Western classical timbre typically uses.

Mix

At higher pitches, where first formant tracking of the second harmonic becomes too effortful or simply no longer possible, strategies vary somewhat. This range is most often referred to as "mix" in the musical theater and commercial music industries, though that term is not without some contention. There is no clear evidence of a neatly delineated, separate laryngeal (muscular) register that can be identified as a mix register, and mix can be executed in either laryngeal register mode one or mode two, depending in part upon range. Whatever the laryngeal component or configuration, there *are* distinctive aural qualities and an ease of production that differentiate it from pure belt while extending speech-like quality higher to about the top of the treble clef. Mix can be identified by expert teachers or judges, which justifies the category of "mix" as at least an acoustic register and strategy.

Strategies for Achieving Mix

Some strategies minimize laryngeal elevation in favor of acoustic and even physical narrowing of articulation (for example, Speech Level Singing) to avoid excessive chestiness and effort. Others utilize adding some degree of nasalance (opening of the nasal port), which can reduce the pressure difference across the glottis (the difference between breath pressure below and above the glottis), moderating the vocal load. Others deliberately avoid nasalance, or at least perceptual nasality. Most all approaches seek to generate sensations of acoustic (vibratory) feedback above the level of the hard palate, rather than continuing the sensation of singing from below up toward the palate, an orientation that the raw yell induces. High, bright, close or semi-close vowels are preferred by most to invite this orientation or "placement" perception. It is most likely that all of these approaches are shifting the resonance from first formant dominance to greater reliance on higher formants resonating higher harmonics for the ringing, bright quality and higher "placement" sensation. The reduction of first formant dominance would also explain the reduction in timbral depth, warmth or roundness. This might be termed, by way of contrast, as a kind of *chiarochiaro* timbre.

Over Vowel Dominance

In terms of the images used in this text, much more dominance of the brightening "over vowel" is called for to achieve both belt and mix qualities. Two ways to avoid recruiting too much breath pressure and glottal resistnace, i.e., "carrying up too much chest," are by narrowing the frontal acoustic sensation to avoid going wider with the vowel sensation, or by using very high close, front vowel shapes with a tongue dorsum that is high enough to cause the sound to seem to originate at and above the hard palate. Bright front vowels, especially /i/, /e/ and /æ/ are typically used to access this production. Maintaining some sense of the two room vocal tract mapping by means of a high tongue dorsum in contact with the upper molars can assist in getting high partial content (ring) with less force or heft. Lowering the tongue dorsum will result in a one room percept, a lower placement percept, and too raw and heavy of a yell response. Some sense of the sensations of the acoustic migratory path of the upper part of the epsilon (see page 48) can assist in getting the tonal sensation above the mouth and palate and into the *masque.* Also increasing awareness of high ring sensation at the top of the back room (near the nasopharynx and TMJs—the top corners of the previously described rectangle image), instead of primarily under the hard palate in the front room, can help to achieve a sense of tonal "placement" above the mouth and minimize laryngeal elevation and compression while still emphasizing upper partial content.

Lateralness Percept

Some belt and mix approaches emphasize lateral width near the top of the vocal tract shape percept in order to emphasize the bright "over vowel" component. Lateral width to the front with perceptual narrowing in the back risks inducing too much laryngeal elevation, too much glottal resistance, and unsustainable pressing. An image that can more safely offer lateral width is conceiving of the belt or mix direction as if ingressive or in reverse, with the perceived lateral width further back, between the temporomandibular joints, rather than primarily at the front of the mouth. That is, conceiving of the sound as if very high and bright but directed inwardly and shaped divergently toward the nasopharynx. Though the actual shape of the lips may still be smile-like and lateral, the acoustic sensation in front is narrower with this image. It tends to encourage a higher tongue dorsum than externally directed, frontal divergence would. It also tends to encourage strong high partial content, preserve higher acoustic vibratory feedback ("placement" perception), reduce the amount of laryngeal elevation necessary, and facilitate less glottal pressing. Another strategy is to use the whisper noise described earlier to experiment with high "bright" noise production that still allows a neutral laryngeal poise or minimal laryngeal elevation. Such a sound will require a smile articulation and a high tongue dorsum, and be perceived as centered in the vicinity of the top of the pharynx (top lateral corners of the back room; the nasopharynx) rather than on the tongue out in the front of the mouth.

Summary

A sustainable, healthy belt or mix will have these characteristics:

- minimal sensation of squeeze at the level of the glottis
- minimal sensation of sub-glottal pressure buildup
- little sense of air "blast" (approaches vary in recommending a percept of low versus high airflow to facilitate low pressure and glottal resistance)
- increased sensation of ease in the neck (compared to the raw yell)
- byproduct sensations of tonal "placement" above the hard palate

- mouth dominant (overvowel) rather than pharynx dominant (undervowel) vowel percept
- unencumbered expressiveness
- speech-like, genuine naturalness, with no false "coloration."

Chapter 8

Summary of Acoustic Objectives and Strategies

Summary of Pedagogic Objectives

Acoustic pedagogy requires knowledge of the acoustic landscape that all singers face. This includes knowledge of the locations and roles of vocal tract resonances, and the effects of interactions between source harmonics and vocal tract resonances. At the very least, learning the contour of first formant locations of the cardinal vowels is essential to effective acoustic pedagogy. Fortunately, that is not difficult.

Acoustic Registration Summarized

Acoustic registration is determined very simply by the relationship of source harmonics with the first formant:

- If two or more harmonics are below the first formant, the singer is in open timbre or *voce aperta.* Said another way, if the singer is more than one octave below the first formant, he or she is in open timbre.
- If only one harmonic is below the first formant, the singer is in close timbre or *voce chiusa.* Said another way, if the singer is within one octave below the first formant, he or she is in close timbre.
- If the first harmonic matches the first formant, the singer is in whoop timbre. Said another way, if the pitch being sung matches the first formant, the singer is in whoop timbre.
- Every time a source harmonic rises through the first formant, there is some degree of timbral closure and vowel migration toward a closer vowel.
- Every time a source harmonic drops below the first formant, there is some degree of timbral opening and vowel migration toward a more open vowel.

Western Classical Singing Objectives

Western classical singing requires a *chiaroscuro* tonal ideal, that balance of depth and brilliance that is beautiful, can project over an orchestra, and is physically sufficiently efficient to be durable and sustainable. It is accomplished by what Sundberg termed a flow phonation and a resonator shaping that results in a healthy singer's formant cluster, at least up to C5. Such a resonator has sufficient convergence to create beneficial acoustic feedback on the vibrator, assisting its efficiency and boosting overall sound output. Such a vocal tract shaping is in fact the open throated poise of historic Italian *bel canto* pedagogy. Therefore a foundational objective of Western classical singing is a technique in which the entire range is produced with an open throat and relatively convergent resonator. This requires:

- A settled larynx
- Uncompressed, possibly even retracted false vocal folds
- A relaxed, fronted tongue
- A lifted soft palate
- Relatively close vowel postures at pitches below the first formant
- Relative independence of tongue and hyoid/larynx structures
- Relative muscular independence of tone generation and vocal tract shape articulation

Most of these objectives must be established before phonation, at the latest during inhalation, and then maintained during the sung phrase, and across all registers and vowel articulations.

Objectives of Acoustic Registration

- All harmonics other than the fundatmental frequency (the sung pitch) should be allowed to pass through the first formant without tracking (without significant shape change).
- This is especially necessary for the second harmonic, whose crossing above the first formant accomplishes the move from open to close timbre (from *voce aperta* to *voca chuisa*).
- Since the first formant locations of vowels span an octave, this acoustic registration event will vary by vowel by as much as an

octave. Most, however, occur within about a perfect fourth, from the turning/closure of the mid close /e/ and /o/ to that of the most open vowel /ɑ/. These closures/turnings are crucial for male passaggio negotiation.

Male Voices (Non-treble)

- An open throated, convergent resonator should be maintained throughout the range.
- Harmonics four and three should pass through the first formant without tracking. This is apparent in the "mini-closures" and vowel migrations that happen with each intersection.
- Maintaining vocal tract shape and convergence in order to maintain first formant locations until the second harmonic passes through the first formant is the gold standard for male passaggio negotiation.
- Unless a head tone float is desired, active vowel modification by vowel opening should be used to raise the first formants of the close vowels (such as /i/ and/u/), keeping them above the sung pitch. This ensures a ringing, virile (chestier) timbre that will match that of the more open vowels.
- A shift in dominance from the first formant to the second may be sought in the upper voice for ringing, climactic top notes. This involves retuning the over vowel to match a higher harmonic (usually the third or fourth harmonic). Care must be taken in this pursuit not to compromise tube length unduly. It is better to pursue this strategy only after a non-pressed phonation and a stable tube length with appropriate and predictable vowel turnings/closures have been established.

Treble Voices

- The lower range of treble voices can be trained acoustically like the passaggio of (non-treble) male voices, as the open vowels migrate into close timbre (*voce chiusa*), even though laryngeal registration will shift from mode one to mode two.
- Maintaining vocal tract shape and convergence in order to main-

tain first formant locations until the sung pitch reaches the first formant and the vowel and timbre migrate into full whoop timbre is the gold standard for treble voices. Vowels achieve maximal migration at full whoop timbre, where the sung pitch matches the first formant. Anticipating, allowing, or even facilitating that migration is necessary.

- Tracking the fundamental frequency (sung pitch) by raising the first formant above its normal location by active vowel modification (vowel opening) is necessary to maintain full whoop timbre.

Vowel Formation and Perception Reviewed

Vowels are a composite of two vowel-like colors created by the harmonics resonated by the first two formants. Awareness of the tone colors of each of these two contributors—the "under vowel" and the "over vowel"—as well as the pitch dependent migrations of the composite timbre acoss acoustic register events, can assist in maintaining an open-throated, convergent resonator and *chiaroscuro* timbre, and in maximizing the mutual support or resonance coupling of the two vowel formants.

Under Vowel Tone Color Awareness

In particular, knowing that the tone color of the "under vowel" is either /u/ or /o/ and occasionally /ɔ/, (which in the case of the front vowels is perceived as a mixture of /u/ or /o/ with the front over vowel quality) assists in maintaining an open throat and appropriately low first formant across range. (See Figure 6, page 37.)

Vowel Migration Anticipation

Furthermore, knowing exactly at which pitch each vowel will close (turn over) for non-treble males, and at which pitch each vowel will reach whoop timbre for treble voices, allows the singer to anticipate the vowel migrations that must occur with those intersections if the throat is to remain settled and open. This is as simple as memorizing the first formant locations of the seven cardinal vowels for a voice, and transposing them as needed from voice type to voice type. (See Figures 8 & 9, pages 59 & 60). These vowel migrations may seem greater to the singer than to the audience.

Pitch Ascent Migration

With pitch ascent, both in the transition into close timbre and into whoop timbre, the percentage of pharyngeally tuned and resonated "under vowel" color will increase in the tonal percept, especially from the point of view of the singer. No step up should be more open in timbre—it is either the same timbre or, more often, closer. No step up should sound more like the "over vowel"—though the *shape* of the intended over vowel should be deliberately maintained, the composite timbre should passively migrate more toward the color of the "under vowel."

Dimenuendo Migration

The "under vowel" percentage will also increase during a diminuendo as higher harmonics weaken relative to the fundamental. The accompanying acoustic sensations will also migrate toward and increasingly center in the vertical pharyngeal column where the "under vowel" is primarily resonated. Resonant quiet tones within treble clef range feel rounder and gently fuller in the pharynx, not smaller. These perceptions accompany a convergent resonator and are necessary in order to maintain an open throat and settled larynx.

Acoustic Sensation Recap

In the case of active modification of the front vowels, as the jaw is opened more, the tongue dorsum kept sufficiently close to the hard palate, the larynx settled, and the throat kept open, perception of the accompanying acoustic sensations will seem to circle behind and below the tongue. It may seem to the singer as if the tongue bulge is "in the way" and that she is singing "through the tongue" rather than having a clear open path over the tongue and out the mouth. With active modification of the open vowels during pitch ascent, the tongue dorsum should seem to float up and the hyoid/larynx to settle downward. This releases them to be further apart, more independent, and to maintain the maximal convergence that the vowel and pitch will allow. Acoustic sensation should seem stronger above and below the mouth, rather than in the mouth.

Conclusion

Motivation for singing must ultimately be simple and, insofar as possible, grounded in unencumbered, sincere expression. The many and varied kinesthetic directives and acoustic perceptions suggested in this text are in the final analysis designed to motivate and maintain an open throated, convergent resonator and to facilitate an efficient, clean, smooth tonal emission across all vowels and registers. Any helpful individual exercises in kinesthetic awareness are intended to be explorations that are rehearsed sufficiently to eventually be incorporated into a single unifying percept. If an effective *chiaroscuro* modality is established, most acoustic register transitions will be subtle, smooth, and will simply take care of themselves. This can certainly be true of those that occur from passive migration. Active modifications may need more special attention, since they involve vocal tract formations that are less innate, diverge further from learned speech patterns, and must therefore first be discovered. However, once identified and rehearsed, even these shape migrations can be subsumed into the general communicative gestalt. In this manner, acoustic voice pedagogy both shares the goals and affirms the strategies of historic Italian *bel canto* pedagogy: freeing the voice for effective, soulful, artistic communication of the human experience.

Appendix I:

Acoustic Designations/Abbreviations

Designations for acoustic elements such as formants and harmonics are not uniform across various voice science disciplines. A recent attempt has been made to come to some agreement in such terminology and their related abbreviations (Titze, et al., 2015). *Practical Vocal Acoustics* made use of designations that were typical in voice-teacher-friendly articles and publications at the time of its publication. Most voice teachers do not need to be concerned with the multiple and somewhat complex factors that concern acoustic science, for which very precise designations are necessary. However, those who seek to go further in their study of voice science need to be aware of current terminology and able to translate simpler terms into their current designations and vice versa.

Below is a conversion of the simplest terms and their designations used in this text.

Harmonics:

H1 = $1f_o$, the first harmonic is the fundamental frequency.
H2 = $2f_o$, the second harmonic is twice the fundamental frequency.
H3 = $3f_o$, the third harmonic is three times the fundamental frequency.
(continuing with H4, H5…)

Formants: there is still no uniform agreement on the definition of the terms vocal tract resonances and vocal tract formants. Most authors that differentiate the terms use resonances to describe attributes of the vocal tract, as in its sound transfer characteristics—the characteristic ways in which it transfers sound from the glottis to the outside world. Those same authors use formants to describe the spectral peaks of the resultant radiated sound. These often differ, since the vocal tract can only resonate harmonics introduced into it by the voice source. If source harmonics do not align exactly with tube resonance peaks, the radiated spectral peaks (formants) will not perfectly match the tube's inherently tuned peaks (resonances). However, most articles and texts addressing singing do not make this distinction and use the term formant to mean a vocal tract characteristic. This text follows that practice.

Formants:

F1 = F_1, the first formant of the vocal tract.

F2 = F_2, the second formant of the vocal tract.

F3 = F_3, the third formant of the vocal tract.

(continuing with F4, F5…)

Formant/Harmonic Interactions

F1/H1 = $F_1{:}1f_o$, the intersection or coupling of the 1st formant with the first harmonic (the sung pitch), which is also called "whoop" coupling. Whoop coupling is maintained in Western classical timbre by raising the first formant above its normal location via vowel opening.

F1/H2 = $F_1{:}2f_o$, the intersection or coupling of the 1st formant with the second harmonic, which event is also the point at which the voice turns over or closes, the point above which close timbre commences and below which open timbre occurs. Maintaining this coupling above the normal first formant location is characteristic of yelling and—if skillfully done—of belting.

F1/H3 = $F_1{:}3f_o$, the intersection of the first formant with the third harmonic, which is relevant to non-treble voices, since there is a "mini-closure" of timbre whenever a source harmonic rises through the first formant. This juncture on the open vowels helps to define the location of the *primo passaggio* in non-treble male voices.

$F_2{:}3f_o$ **or** $F_2{:}4f_o$, the intersection or coupling of the 2nd formant with the third or fourth harmonic, a strategy used to increase the ring and power of male upper voice in Western classical singing, and possibly also as a strategy in high belt timbre.

Appendix II:

Definitions

Absolute spectral tone color: the characteristic of individual frequencies to be perceived by humans as having a specific vowel-like quality. For example, low frequency harmonics have an /u/ like quality; high frequencies have an /i/ like quality. Vowels are perceived to be a combination of the absolute spectral tone colors of the harmonics being reinforced by the first and second formants of the vocal tract. This approximation of a vowel quality is indicated by a tilde plus the vowel.

Acoustic registration: the timbral transitions that occur as a result of harmonic:formant interactions. All acoustic register events involve harmonic interactions with the first formant. Many also involve interaction with the second formant.

Affect: emotive expression, important for spontaneous motivation and maintenance of pharyngeal postures and necessary for vocal tract stability across range and vowels.

Articulation: in speech and singing, the shaping or tuning of the vocal tract to modify the filtered voice source signal. Articulation also includes how the tongue, lips, jaw, and other speech organs are involved in the production of consonant sounds.

Belting: a singing style with a mode one-dominant laryngeal registration, using an acoustic strategy in which the first formant tracks the second harmonic; in other words, a kind of skillful, artistic yelling. Some form of belt is prevalent in many forms of popular, folk, and world music and in American musical theater. For pitches above mode one, a resonance strategy is used to reinforce higher partials to extend a belt-like, bright timbre into the top of the treble clef and above.

Body mapping: an offshoot of Alexander Technique, postulating that we each have an internal conceptual map of how the body is put together and functions. An accurate map is thought to lead to coordinated function, but a faulty map to awkward function.

Capital C image: a description of the path of acoustic sensations, in which higher pitches bifurcate into two rounded sensory paths back up and over the palate, and back down and under the tongue and jaw.

Chiaroscuro: an Italian term meaning "bright-dark" borrowed from art history to describe an ideal resonance balance between low and high frequency components in Western classical singing. It is usually accomplished (in middle and lower ranges) by some balance in power between the first formant and the singer's formant cluster.

Close timbre: a vocal sound in which the second harmonic has risen above the first formant, causing the voice to "turn over." Also termed *voce chiusa* in Italian.

Close vowel: a vowel with a low first formant such as /i/ and /u/ and an inherently convergent resonator shape.

Convergent resonator: a vocal tract shape that is relatively (for the vowel being produced) more open near the glottis and narrower near the lips (the inverted megaphone). Such a resonance strategy is typical of Western classical singing and *voce chiusa.*

Cover: the timbral shift that accompanies the $F_1{:}2f_0$ crossing; turning over.

Depth: a description of the timbre of a sound that has significant strength in one of its lower harmonics, as resonated by the first formant.

Divergent resonator: a description of a resonator shape that is smaller in the pharynx and more open nearer the lips. Open vowels are inherently divergent in shape. This resonance strategy is typical of musical theater as well as many world music singing styles.

Downstream resister: any resister (articulator position or device that resists airflow to some extent) that is downstream from the vocal folds, i.e., nearer to or at the lips, such as a lip "brr," lip tongue "raspberry," or tongue trill. Downstream resisters share the pressure load from the lungs with the vocal folds, necessitating higher airflow through the glottis and reducing the pressure difference across the vocal folds. This inhibits pressing. Some authors refer to downstream resisters as a subset of semi-occluded vocal tract. (See also **Semi-occluded vocal tract**.)

Epsilon image: a description of the path of acoustic sensations, in which the lower middle voice rings more in the mouth on the hard palate like the middle "leg" of the epsilon, while higher pitches bifurcate into two rounded paths back up and over the palate, and back down and under the tongue and jaw.

Formant: a natural resonance of the vocal tract, caused by standing waves in the quarter wave resonator.

> **Vowel formants:** the first (lowest) two formants of the vocal tract are also the most tunable, and therefore the most significant in defining the vowel quality of a sound. Together they are called the vowel formants.
>
> **Singer's formant cluster:** a clustering of formants three and above (usually formants 3-5) generated by a low larynx, open laryngopharynx, and narrowed epilaryngeal tube exit, that results in an increase in power in the high frequency components of a sung sound. It is especially characteristic of males in Western classical singing, enabling them to carry over orchestral accompaniment.

Formant detuning: the tuning of a formant frequency peak away from a harmonic to weaken its effect. Used with F2 in female/treble upper range to reduce shrillness and with F1 in males voices to avoid whoop timbre on close vowels.

Formant tracking: the tuning of a formant to follow or track a specific harmonic, such as F_1:$1f_0$ tracking of whoop timbre (upper female voice strategy) or F_1:$2f_0$ tracking of the yell or of belting.

Formant tuning: the tuning of one or both of the first two formants in order to find a better formant:harmonic match for greater resonance.

Front-back dimension: a description either of a physical articulatory characteristic (a fronted tongue hump versus a tongue hump further back), or of an acoustic characteristic (a sound with a high second formant and therefore stronger high partials, i.e., a front vowel; or a low second formant and therefore weaker high partials and potentially stronger low partials, i.e., a back vowel).

Fullness: a typical descriptor of a sound with significant strength in its lowest harmonics, as resonated by the first formant. Other similar terms are: depth, warmth, roundness.

Fundamental frequency ($1f_0$): the lowest harmonic of a sound (H1 or $1f_0$), more or less equivalent to the perceived pitch.

Glottal suction therapy: a therapy in which the glottis is closed, inhalatory effort is activated, sucking the glottis and larynx downward. Since, with the exception of the glottal closure, the action is inhalatory, it is thought to open the throat and stretch the thyrohyoid space from below without activating contraction around the larynx that typically accompanies exhalatory glottal compression.

Harmonic: a frequency component of a sound. Harmonic frequency components are either the lowest component (the fundamental frequency) or whole integer multiples of the lowest frequency component. Together they therefore generate a pressure waveform that repeats at the frequency of that lowest common denominator.

Heavy cover: deliberate lowering of F_1 (by tube lengthening and vowel closing) to precipitate the turning over of the voice. Strategies used include lowering the larynx, lip rounding and/or trumpeting, and vowel darkening.

Kinesthesia: a person's sensory awareness of how body parts are situated, how joints are articulated, and how movement functions.

Laryngeal register: the muscular adjustment of the vocal folds; the relative participation of the thryoarytenoid (TA—shortening, thickening) muscles and the cricothyroid (CT—stretching, thinning) muscles.

> **Chesty:** historic description of a sound long assumed to have greater TA activation and vocal process adduction, with shorter, thicker, looser vocal folds, and shallower spectral tilt, with stronger high harmonic component frequencies. Now called vibrational **mode one**.

Heady: historic description of a sound long assumed to have less TA and greater CT activation, with thinner, longer, tauter vocal folds, and a stronger fundamental and steeper spectral tilt with fewer and weaker high harmonic component frequencies. Now called vibrational **mode two**.

Mode one (M1): a vibrational mode of the voice source in which the vocal fold shape is short and thick, and the vocal fold cover loose. It has **vertical phase difference**, generating more and stronger high partials. (See **Laryngeal register**.)

Mode two (M2): a vibrational mode of the voice source in which the vocal fold shape is long and thin, and the vocal fold cover is taut. It has little **vertical phase difference**, resulting in a more sinusoidal pressure wave that is more fundamental frequency dominant. Thought to be caused by greater CT laryngeal muscle participation and usually passive TAs. (See **Laryngeal register**.)

Openness-closeness dimension: descriptions of a vocal sound relative to the frequency location of its first formant and to the relationship of its harmonics to its first formant. (See ***Voce chiusa*, Close timbre, Close vowel,** and ***Voce aperta*, Open timbre, Open vowel.**)

Open timbre: a vocal sound in which two or more harmonics are at or below the first formant of the vowel being sung. Also termed *voce aperta* in Italian. Sometimes also used to describe a generally divergent resonance shape strategy.

Open vowel: a vowel with a high first formant, such as /ɑ/, and an inherently divergent resonator shape.

Partial: a spectral component of sound, like a harmonic or overtone. Partials can be harmonic (whole integer multiples of the fundamental frequency) or not.

Passaggio: Italian for passage or transition into the upper voice.

Primo passaggio: the lower entry into the transition zone.

Secondo passaggio: the upper exit of the transition zone, entry into the upper voice.

Zona di passaggio: the transition zone, a range segment of about a 4th or 5th in males, during which glottal adjustments are needed to minimize increases in subglottal pressure or glottal resitance, and the acoustic register changes from open to close timbre for most vowels. In females, this transition area is longer and is subdivided into a lower middle and upper middle, during which the voice transions into vibrational mode 2.

Passive vowel modification: this author's proposed designation for a change in vowel quality accomplished by retaining the vocal tract shape but moving the pitch with its set of harmonics. The change in vowel quality results from the changing relationships and interactions between the stable formants and the moving harmonics. (See **Vowel modification.**)

Pitch: our perception of the frequency of a sound. It is the frequency of the composite pressure pattern of the multiple frequencies of a tone. In most practical circumstances, it can be considered the equivalent of the fundamental frequency.

Pitch of turning: the pitch at which a voice turns over, just inside of an octave below the pitch of the first formant of the vowel being sung; the pitch at which the $2f_0$ crosses above the F_1 of the vowel being sung.

Pre-phonatory tuning: the shaping of the vocal tract prior to phonation, usually during inhalation; the "tuning" of the resonances of the vocal tract prior to phonation.

Primary acoustic register transitions: prominent acoustic registration events at the point at which $2f_0$ crosses F_1, transitioning from open to close timbre, and the point at which $1f_0$ intersects F_1, attaining whoop timbre. Refining these two events is a major goal of Western classical singing pedagogy for non-treble and treble voices, respectively. The former is most often associated with the turning over of the open vowels in the neighborhood of C4-G4 in male voices. The latter is the preferred strategy for the upper range of Western classical female and treble voice singing.

Primary laryngeal register transition: the shift from chest to falsetto, or vibrational mode one to vibrational mode two. Male classical singers tend to avoid this shift, staying in some form of mode one for the entire range. Female classical singers tend to shift from mode one to mode two between C4 and G4, usually before (below) the F_1:$2f_o$ acoustic register transition. Belters extend mode one or chest register to ca. C5.

Resonance: Resonance is the tendency of an object or system to respond (oscillate) more strongly to particular frequencies introduced into it.

Speech Level Singing (SLS): a pedagogic approach initiated by Seth Riggs, and currently disseminated by several independent international groups (IVA, IVTOM, etc.).

Semi-occluded vocal tract: a vocal tract with an exit sufficiently narrowed to generate flow resistance or acoustic impedance. A short thin straw is one mechanical example. A very small, kazoo-like /w/ is an articulatory example. (See also **Downstream resister**.)

Spectral centroid: an amplitude weighted average of the spectral components of a resonance area. For example, a vocal tract formant (resonance) may be amplifying several harmonics. The cumulative effect of those harmonics on the perceived absolute tone color (vowel-like quality) can be determined by calculating their spectral centroid. In a simple example, two adjacent, amplified harmonics with equal amplitudes will generate a color percept of a phantom harmonic between them. If one harmonic is stronger than the other, that phantom harmonic percept would be closer to the absolute tone color of the stronger harmonic.

Temporomandibular joint (TMJ): the joints of the jaw with the skull, just in front of the ear canals. A handy reference for sensations of palatal height and over vowel ring.

Turning over: the passing of $2f_o$ above F_1 of a voice, and its accompanying sound and sensation.

Voce aperta: open timbre; any sung sounds in which two or more harmonics are at or below the first formant—in other words, the timbre of any pitches sung an octave or more below the first formant. This term has also been used historically to describe an overall divergent resonator shape characterized by open timbre, in which vowels tend to spread and move into yell timbre, and more typical of belting and various world music singing styles.

Voce chiusa: close timbre; any sung sounds in which the second harmonic is above the first formant—in other words, the timbre of any pitches within an octave below the first formant. This term has also been used historically to describe an overall convergent resonator poise that results in the *chiaroscuro* timbre of Western classical singing, in which vowels close when and where they should, in contrast to a predominantly divergent, open timbre resonator adjustment.

Voice source: the sound signal produced at the vibrator (vocal folds).

Vowel formants: (see **Formant**.)

Vowel modification: historically understood to refer to a change in the vowel quality accomplished by moving the vowel formants from their normal speech locations by means of changes in the shape of the vocal tract in an attempt to find better (more resonant) formant:harmonic matches. This text proposes the subcategories: active and passive vowel modification. (See **Passive vowel modification**.)

Vowel migration: another term for passive vowel modification; the gradual timbral change a vowel undergoes when vocal tract shape is maintained while pitch is changed; due to the changing relationships between stable formants and changing harmonics, especially evident when harmonics pass through the first formant.

Whoop: also called "hoot" (D. Miller); the timbre that occurs when singing the pitch of the first formant, or when the first formant is tracking the pitch one is singing. Acoustically, its radiated spectrum has a rather dominant first harmonic. In its unrefined form, it is rather "hooty" and can be accompanied by excessive tongue backing.

Yell coupling, yell timbre: an acoustic coupling of F_1 and $2f_0$ that has been carried higher than normal through tube shortening and mouth widening (F_1:$2f_0$ tracking); bright and often pressed and spread in quality.

Selected References

Austin, Stephen F. "The *voce chiusa.*" *Journal of Singing.* March/April 2005; Vol. 61, No. 4: 421-425.

Austin, Stephen F. "From Song to Speech: Nasal Resonance-Fact or Fiction?" *Journal of Singing* November/December 2000, vol. 57, no. 2: 33-41.

Austin, Stephen F. "Movement of the Velum During Speech and Singing in Classically Trained Singers." *Journal of Voice* vol 11, no.2 (June 1997); 212-221

Bauer, Karen. *The Essentials of Beautiful Singing: A Three-Step Kinesthetic Approach.* Scarecrow: 2013.

Bloem-Hubatka, Daniela. *The Old Italian School of Singing.* McFarland & Company, Inc.: 2012

Bourne, T., Garnier, M., Kenny, D. "Music Theater Voice: Production, Physiology and Pedagogy." *Journal of Singing.* March/April 2011; Vol 67, No. 4: 237-244.

Bozeman, Kenneth. "A Case for Voice Science in the Voice Studio." *Journal of Singing.* Jan/Feb 2007; Vol. 63, No. 3:265–270.

Bozeman, Kenneth. "Acoustic *passaggio* pedagogy for the male voice." *Logopedics Phoniatrics Vocology.* 2012 Early Online. 1-6.

Bozeman, Kenneth. "On the Voice: Registration Strategies for Training the Male *Passaggio.*" *Choral Journal.* June/July, 2008; 48:59-72.

Bozeman, Kenneth. "The Role of the First Formant in Training the Male Singing Voice." *Journal of Singing.* Jan/Feb 2010; Vol. 66, No. 3:291-297.

Bozeman, Kenneth. "Remapping the Open Throat (Gola Aperta)." *Journal of Singing.* Nov/Dec 2015; Vol. 72, No. 2:183-187.

Bozeman, Kenneth, "Studio Metaphors for Acoustic Pedagogy," VOICE*Prints,* The Journal of the New York Singing Teachers' Association, March/April 2016, pp.4-6.

Herbst, Christian T., Howard, David, Švec, Jan G. "The sound source in singing—basic principles and muscular adjustments for fine-tuning vocal timbre." in: *The Oxford Handbook of Singing*. Oxford University Press, D. Howard, J. Nix, G. Welch Eds.

Howell, Ian, "Parsing the Spectral Envelope: Toward a General Theory of Vocal Tone Color." DMA thesis, New England Conservatory of Music, 2016. Retrieved from https://www.academia.edu/29162454.

Ladefoged, Peter. *Elements of acoustic phonetics*, Chicago, Il: University of Chicago Press: 1962.

Lovetri, Jeanette. "The Confusion about Belting: a Personal Observation." *VoicePrints: Journal of the New York Singing Teachers' Association* September-October 2012, pp. 4-7.

McCoy, Scott. *Your Voice, An Inside View,* Gahanna, OH: Inside View-Press: 2012.

McKinney, James. *The Diagnosis and Correction of Vocal Faults.* San Diego, CA: Singular Press: 1982.

Miller, Donald G. *Registers of the Singing Voice,* Groningen, Netherlands: Groningen Press: 2000.

Miller, Donald G. *Resonance in Singing*, Princeton, NJ: Inside View Press: 2008.

Miller, Richard. *The Structure of Singing: System and Art in Vocal Technique.* New York: Schirmer Books: 1986.

Perna, Nicholas. "Nasalance and the Tenor Passiaggo." *Journal of Singing,* March/April 2014, Vol. 70 no. 4: 403-410

Perna, Nicholas. *The Effects of Nasalance on the Acoustics of the Tenor Passaggio and Head Voice.* Dissertation; University of Miami Scholarly Repository, April 21, 2008.

Schutte, Harm K., Miller, Donald, G. "Belting and Pop, Nonclassical Approaches to Female Middle Voice: Some Preliminary Considerations." *Journal of Voice.* 7(2) (1993): 142-150.

Stark, James. *Bel Canto: A History of Vocal Pedagogy.* University of Toronto Press: 2000.

Steinhauer, Kimberly M., and Estill, Jo. "The Estill Voice Model: Physiology of Emotion," *Voice and Emotion*, Vol. 2, Chapter 6, Plural Publishing; 2008. pp 83-99.

Sundberg, Johan. "Articulatory interpretation of the singing formants," *Journal of the Acoustical Society of America,* 55 (1974): 838 –844.

Sundberg, Johan, et al. "Velum Behavior in Professional Classic Operatic Singing." *Journal of Voice* vol. 16, no. 1 (March 2002): 61-71

Sundberg, Johan. *The Science of the Singing Voice*, Imprint DeKalb, Ill.: Northern Illinois University Press: 1987.

Trimble, Michael. *Fundamentals of Great Vocal Technique.* Inside View Press: 2015.

Titze, Ingo. *Principles of Voice Production*, Englewood Cliffs, N.J.: Prentice Hall: 1994.

Titze, Ingo., & Story, Brad. "Acoustic interactions of the voice source with the lower vocal tract," *Journal of the Acoustical Society of America*, 101(4) (1997): 2234-2243.

Titze, Ingo, et al. " Toward a consensus on symbolic notation of harmonics, resonances, and formants in vocalization," *The Journal of the Acoustical Society of America*, 137(5), May 2015: 3005-7.

End Notes

Chapter 2

---

[i] Richard Miller, *The Structure of Singing* (New York: Schirmer Books/MacMillan, 1986), 58.

[ii] Helen F. Mitchell, Dianna T. Kenny, "Open Throat: Acoustic and Perceptual Support for Pedagogic Practice," *Journal of Singing* 61 no. 4 (March/April 2008): 429–441.

[iii] Stephen Austin, "The *voce chiusa*," *Journal of Singing* 61 no. 4 (March/April 2005): 421–426.

[iv] Miller, 58-59.

[v] Miller, 60.

[vi] From a private conversation with Per-Åke Lindestad, Swedish laryngologist and specialist in laryngeal and pharyngeal anatomy.

[vii] Ingo Titze, "Why do Classically Trained Singers Widen Their Throat?" *Journal of Singing* 69, no. 2 (November/December 2012): 177-178.

[viii] Kenneth Bozeman, *Practical Vocal Acoustics: Pedagogic Applications for Teachers and Singers.* (Hillsdale, NY: Pendragon Press, 2013), 17-18.

[ix] Johan Sundburg, "Articulatory interpretation of the singing formants," *Journal of the Acoustical Society of America* 55 (1974): 838 – 844.

[x] Ingo Titze, Brad Story, "Acoustic interactions of the voice source with the lower vocal tract," *Journal of the Acoustical Society of America* 101(4) (1997): 2234-2243.

[xi] Kimberly M. Steinhauer, Jo Estill, "The Estill Voice Model: Physiology of Emotion," *Voice and Emotion*, Vol. 2, Chapter 6, (Plural Publishing, 2008), 83-99.

[xii] Bozeman, 60-61.

[xiii] Ibid., 61.